The Russian Federation: Then and Now

John Allen

About the Author

John Allen is a writer who lives in Oklahoma City. He has long been interested in Russia, its literature, and its political changes.

© 2015 ReferencePoint Press, Inc.
Printed in the United States

For more information, contact:
ReferencePoint Press, Inc.
PO Box 27779
San Diego, CA 92198
www.ReferencePointPress.com

Picture Credits:
Cover: Steve Zmina; Akg-images/Newscom: 52; Design Pics/Christopher Roberts/Newscom: 56; © Hulton-Deutsch Collection/Corbis: 27; © Sergei Karpukhin/Reuters/Corbis: 32; © Sergei Ilnitsky/epa/Corbis: 65; © Jerome Levitch/Corbis: 35; © Cody Marsh/National Geographic Society/Corbis: 39; © Christopher J. Morris/Corbis: 61; © Michael Nicholson/Corbis: 16; © Alfredo Dalgi Orti/The Art Archive/Corbis: 48; © Anton Pedko/epa/Corbis: 8; © Pierre Perrin/Sygma/Corbis: 23; Thinkstock Images: 4, 5; © Peter Turnley/Corbis: 43; © Shamil Zhumatov/Reuters/Corbis: 68; Steve Zmina: 12

LIBRARY OF CONGRESS CATALOGING-IN-PUBLICATION DATA

Allen, John, 1957–
  The Russian Federation : then and now / by John Allen.
      pages cm. — (The former Soviet Union: then and now series)
  Audience: Grades 9-12.
  Includes bibliographical references and index.
  ISBN-13: 978-1-60152-692-2 (hardback)
  ISBN-10: 1-60152-692-X (hardback)
  1. Russia (Federation)—History—Juvenile literature. 2. Soviet Union—History—Juvenile literature. 3. Russia (Federation)—Politics and government—Juvenile literature. 4. Soviet Union—Politics and government—Juvenile literature. I. Title.
  DK510.56.A55 2015
  947.086—dc23
                                                                            2014003310

CONTENTS

IMPORTANT EVENTS IN THE RUSSIAN FEDERATION: THEN AND NOW

1917
In February Czar Nicholas II steps down and is replaced by the Provisional Government, led by Alexander Kerensky.

1936
Stalin begins the Great Terror, a thorough purge of all those he considers to be enemies of the people.

1921
In March the party adopts the New Economic Policy, a moderate program that replaces the much harsher War Communism and leads to expansion of industry and agriculture.

1944
The Red Army is able to end the Siege of Leningrad, in which Nazi troops had encircled the city for almost three years. This event led to Soviet victory in World War II.

1925   1930   1935   1940   1945

1929
Stalin announces his plan to eliminate the wealthier peasants, called *kulaks*, as a class. This policy leads to a deliberately created famine throughout the countryside of Russia and the other Soviet republics.

1945
Soviet troops occupy most of Eastern and Central Europe, greatly expanding the Soviet bloc of nations.

1946
Former British prime minister Winston Churchill describes Soviet control of Eastern Europe as an iron curtain descending over the region, which initiates the Cold War between the Soviet bloc and the West.

1924
On January 21 Lenin dies, prompting the party to venerate him as a symbol of the revolution. His successors, including Josef Stalin, begin a rivalry for power that will end with Stalin in charge.

1918
On July 17 Czar Nicholas II and his family are murdered by members of the Ural soviet (workers' council), ostensibly to keep them from being freed by White Army troops.

1917
In October the Bolsheviks, led by Vladimir Lenin, seize power and establish a Communist dictatorship.

2014
The Russian Federation hosts its first Winter Olympics, which take place in the Black Sea town of Sochi. On February 27 Russian troops seize control of Crimea, a peninsula in southern Ukraine. The takeover follows months of protests in Ukraine, which culminated in the ouster of President Viktor Yanukovych, who had close ties with the Russian Federation.

2012
Putin is elected to a third term as president of the Russian Federation after serving as prime minister for one term, during which he ruled the nation jointly with President Dmitry Medvedev.

1956
Nikita Khrushchev delivers a secret speech to the Twentieth Congress of the Communist Party in which he acknowledges some of Stalin's crimes against the nation; Red Army tanks enter Budapest, Hungary, to suppress an uprising of workers and students seeking an end to Soviet rule.

1999
On December 31 Vladimir Putin becomes acting president of the Russian Federation when Yeltsin resigns. A few months later Putin is elected to the presidency.

1985
The Politburo chooses the relatively young Mikhail Gorbachev to be the new Soviet general secretary. Gorbachev's reforms, called *glasnost* and *perestroika*, attempted to restructure Soviet society.

1960   **1970**   **1980**   **1990**   **2000**

1968
In a November 13 speech to the Polish Workers' Party, Soviet leader Leonid Brezhnev announces the Brezhnev Doctrine, a policy of defending socialist states that is used to justify the Soviet invasion of Czechoslovakia three months earlier.

1989
On November 9 East German authorities allow their citizens to travel freely to West Berlin. The fall of the Berlin Wall separating East Germany from the West indicates that Soviet control of its satellite nations is at an end.

2013
On December 19 Putin authorizes the release of Mikhail Khodorkovsky, a political foe imprisoned since 2003. Many observers assume Putin wants to improve the Russian state's image prior to the 2014 Winter Olympics in Sochi.

1991
In December the Soviet Union breaks up into fifteen separate countries, the largest and most powerful of which is the Russian Federation, led by Boris Yeltsin.

The Russian Federation

In July 2013 the Russian Federation granted temporary asylum to Edward Snowden, an American computer specialist with the National Security Agency. Snowden had leaked information to the press about top secret US surveillance programs, and the American government was urging that Snowden be handed over for trial on charges of espionage and theft. Russian president Vladimir Putin had initially sounded sympathetic to American concerns. "If [Snowden] wants to stay here," said Putin, "there is one condition: he must stop his activities aimed at inflicting damage to our American partners, no matter how strange it may sound on my lips."[1] Yet Putin, emphasizing that Russia had no extradition agreement with the United States, coolly continued to deny Washington's requests for Snowden's return and finally gave him official refuge.

Two months later Russia and the United States were at odds again, this time over Syria's reported use of chemical weapons against rebels in that country. Syria had long been a client state of Russia. With the United States threatening military strikes against Syria, Putin this time negotiated a settlement in which Syrian president Bashar al-Assad agreed to destroy his chemical weapons and submit to inspections.

In late February 2014 tensions ratcheted even higher. Armed troops from Russia seized control of Crimea, a peninsula in southern Ukraine. This followed a turbulent month during which massive street protests in Kiev, the Ukrainian capital, led to the ouster of President Victor Yanukovych, a politician with close ties to Russia. Pressured by Putin and his occupying troops, Crimean leaders held a referendum on joining the Russian

Federation, a vote that resulted in overwhelming support for the move. US President Barack Obama, along with many world leaders, condemned the invasion and sudden referendum as clear violations of international law.

Echoes of the Cold War

Together these incidents highlighted Putin's intention to return Russia to a leading role in world affairs. Onlookers were reminded of the Cold War antagonism between the former Soviet Union, which was dominated by Russia, and the United States. According to former US secretary of defense Robert M. Gates, "Mr. Putin aspires to restore Russia's global power and influence and to bring the now-independent states that were once part of the Soviet Union back into Moscow's orbit. . . . There is no grand plan or strategy to do this, just opportunistic and ruthless aspiration. And patience."[2]

Echoes of the Cold War and Soviet assertiveness are just one more example of Putin's authoritarian approach to governing. Under his rule, Russia has slipped back toward autocracy and concentrated wealth among a new elite. While lip service is paid to democracy, true power is reserved for the *silnaya ruka*, or iron fist, of centralized control. In this view Putin is merely one more in a long line of autocrats, whether they were called czars, general secretaries, or presidents. Opinion polls regularly find that a majority of Russians accept the need for concentrating power in a strong leader. Some older Russians still mourn the demise of the Soviet Union, in which the state made all the important decisions about jobs, housing, culture, and communication. The personal freedom taken for granted in many Western nations has been a hard lesson for many Russians to learn in the last quarter century. The result has been a society—and an economy—mired in cronyism, corruption, and a frequently cynical attitude about what it takes to get ahead.

> "Mr. Putin aspires to restore Russia's global power and influence and to bring the now-independent states that were once part of the Soviet Union back into Moscow's orbit."[2]
>
> —Former US secretary of defense Robert M. Gates.

Crimea's large ethnic Russian population celebrates Russia's annexation of Crimea in March 2014. The action by Russian Federation president Vladimir Putin widened political divisions within Ukraine and brought condemnation from world leaders.

A Nation in Transition

Despite these societal ills, there have been undeniable successes in the Russian Federation. With help from its vast resources of oil and natural gas, Russia's economy has grown almost every year since Putin was first elected in March 2000. The standard of living for most Russians has generally improved, although average incomes are low and recent figures show signs of stagnation. Freedom of expression, while still limited in some ways, is much more robust than under the Soviet regime. Long-standing Russian problems that have been well publicized in the West—such as rampant alcoholism and an alarming decline in birthrates—still exist but are showing a more positive trend. Mark Adomanis, an expert on Russian economics and demographics, sees a need for more balanced reporting. "Part of what gets me so frustrated about most mainstream media coverage of Russia," Adomanis explained, "is that people tend to conflate the country's condition (e.g., people drink a lot, don't make much money, and are generally miserable) with its trajectory (e.g., people are drinking *more*, people are making *less* money, and people are getting *more* miserable). These are, obviously, two very different things, but they're often treated as if they're interchangeable."[3]

Putin himself believes that the Western media is biased in its reporting on Russia. Yet his actions merely provide new evidence of his push for control. On December 9, 2013, the Russian president shut down the state news agency RIA Novosti and replaced it with a new group led by a fiery pro-Kremlin manager. (The Kremlin, a complex of palaces in Moscow, is Russia's version of the US White House.) RIA Novosti had angered Putin with its coverage of protests against him. The move demonstrates that the Russian Federation remains a country in transition, still struggling to escape its autocratic past.

CHAPTER ONE

The October Revolution

"We shall now proceed to construct the socialist order!"[4] These first words delivered by Vladimir Lenin to the Congress of Soviets on October 26, 1917, reflected the spirit of confidence and optimism that greeted the Bolshevik takeover of the Russian government. Very soon the euphoria would turn to apprehension. Revolutionaries who had scarcely run anything other than party meetings now had the reins of government and no expertise in governing. Lenin quickly demonstrated his ruthlessness. From the confiscation of private property and the nationalization of most industries to the creation of a secret police force, Lenin and the Bolsheviks focused on tightening their iron grip on the country. The political atmosphere in Russia underwent a radical change that would last more than seventy years.

A Window to Europe

The history of Russia leading up to the October Revolution is a story of tyranny interrupted by brief periods of enlightenment and reform. In land area Russia is the largest country in the world. Its area of more than 6.5 million square miles (17 million sq. km) is almost twice that of the next largest country, Canada. The task of ruling this vast and ethnically diverse country—it includes one-eighth of earth's inhabited land—was undertaken by a series of tyrants going back centuries. The ruler of Russia was traditionally called "czar," which is the Russian derivation of *Caesar*. The first "czar of all the Russias" was Ivan the Terrible, crowned in 1547. Known for his temper and ruthlessness, Ivan conquered neighboring lands, including Siberia, and transformed Russia into a multiethnic empire. He also sponsored the first code of laws in Russia and set up a feudal assembly. In essence Ivan was the first "strongman" ruler of Russia, initiating a despotic, centralized political structure that historians agree was the basis of autocracy going forward.

Following a chaotic period known as the "Time of Troubles," the Romanov dynasty rose to power. The first significant Romanov czar was Peter the Great, who ruled Russia from 1682 until his death in 1725. A giant for his time at 6 feet 8 inches (203 cm), Peter further expanded the Russian Empire with a series of military conquests and also established new ties of trade and culture with Europe. It was his goal to hack through a window on Europe (a phrase that originated with the poet Alexander Pushkin), looking westward for cultural inspiration. Peter also built the city of Saint Petersburg on swampy terrain in the northwest of Russia and made it the new capital. German-born Catherine the Great, who ruled from 1762 to 1796, was even more emphatic in her interest in European ideas and customs. Under Catherine, Russia's military might and prestige continued to expand until the country came to be viewed as one of Europe's great powers.

> "I have taken precaution to avoid witnessing these cruel proceedings, but they occur so often, they are so habitual in the villages, that it is impossible to avoid hearing the cries of the unfortunate victims of inhuman caprice."[5]
>
> —An eighteenth-century French visitor to Russia, remarking on whippings as punishment.

Although historians generally characterize Catherine's reign as an enlightened despotism (exercise of absolute power), the period also saw conditions grow worse for many Russian serfs—peasants bound to large landowners in a relationship close to slavery. A French visitor to Russia remarked on the widespread whippings and casual cruelty: "I have taken precaution to avoid witnessing these cruel proceedings, but they occur so often, they are so habitual in the villages, that it is impossible to avoid hearing the cries of the unfortunate victims of inhuman caprice. Their cries followed me in dreams."[5] Occasionally, serfs would threaten to revolt at their inhumane

The Russian Federation

treatment. Pugachev's Rebellion in 1774, an early example of a popular uprising against Russian authority, showed the depth of discontentment among not only peasants but also many other groups in imperial Russia.

The Russian Intelligentsia

Revolutionary violence erupted again in 1825 when upper-class military officers called the Decembrists (for the month in which the rebellion took place) revolted against the newly installed Czar Nicholas I. The Decembrists sought to replace the czarist system with a constitutional government. Troops loyal to Nicholas suppressed the rebellion, and the rebel leaders were executed and their followers exiled to Siberia. Yet the Decembrists became martyrs to the cause of liberalization and proved inspirational to later dissidents and revolutionaries. A loose framework of dissidents from all levels of society, including doctors, lawyers, factory workers, teachers, students, engineers, scientists, and writers, made up the Russian intelligentsia. These individuals had a shared disgust of the entrenched evils of czarism and desperately wanted to bring a new spirit of freedom to their country. But as Russian writers Fyodor Dostoyevsky, Anton Chekhov, and others noted, most of these intellectuals dreamed of bringing about change but had no idea where to begin.

Among the intelligentsia other dissidents arose who were more inclined to act. Political violence in nineteenth-century Russia gave the czarist regime excuses to crush all dissent. For example, in 1866, five years after Alexander II had freed the serfs and begun to institute many other liberal reforms, a member of a revolutionary group tried but failed to assassinate the czar with a bomb in the street. The attempt led to a predictable backlash as Alexander quashed all hopes for further political reforms. Thirteen years later another assassin from a terrorist group called the People's Will succeeded in killing Alexander. In the paranoid atmosphere that followed, czarist agents looked everywhere for signs of radical political leanings. As a result, intellectuals seeking change either kept silent or continued their work together in underground organizations.

Lenin and the Bolsheviks

One such subversive intellectual was named Vladimir Ilyich Ulyanov. A bright student from Simbirsk, a city on the Volga River, Ulyanov had become radicalized after his brother was executed for participating in an assassination plot against Alexander III. Thrown out of school because of his brother's crimes, Ulyanov seethed with resentment against the czarist regime that had spoiled his career and the bourgeois (middle-class) liberals who had shunned his family. Thus, it was not sympathy for the plight of the poor or solidarity with workers that originally inspired Ulyanov's revolutionary fire. Taking the name Lenin, Ulyanov threw himself into radical politics and almost immediately was arrested and exiled to Siberia for three years. There he continued his detailed study of Marxism, the utopian socialist philosophy of the German Karl Marx. Lenin adapted Marx's philosophy to suit his own revolutionary ideas. Lenin's main fear was that other socialist parties, which were rapidly gaining followers in Russia, were too ready to compromise with bourgeois oppressors such

Lenin on Democracy

The Soviet Union's official ideology was Marxism. The German philosopher Karl Marx (1818–1883) believed that capitalism was an immoral system that allowed the property-owning class to exploit the working class. Lenin studied Marx and added his own ideas about how postrevolutionary society should be organized. In this excerpt from a speech delivered December 23, 1918, Lenin warns his listeners about trusting too much in democracy.

It is sheer mockery of the working and exploited people to speak of pure democracy, of democracy in general, of equality, freedom and universal rights when the workers and all working people are ill-fed, ill-clad, ruined and worn out, not only as a result of capitalist wage slavery, but as a consequence of four years of predatory war, while the capitalists and profiteers remain in possession of the "property" usurped by them and the "ready-made" apparatus of state power. This is tantamount to trampling on the basic truths of Marxism which has taught the workers: you must take advantage of bourgeois democracy which, compared with feudalism, represents a great historical advance, but not for one minute must you forget the bourgeois character of this "democracy," its historical, conditional and limited character. Never share the "superstitious belief" in the "state" and never forget that the state even in the most democratic republic, and not only in a monarchy, is simply a machine for the suppression of one class by another.

Vladimir Ilich Lenin, "'Democracy' and Dictatorship," transcript, *Historical Speeches* (blog), WordPress, November 2, 2008. http://greatspeeches.wordpress.com.

as factory owners by forming trade unions and settling for better working conditions. By contrast, Lenin never deviated from his goal of overthrowing the czarist regime. It was this relentless fanaticism that led to his success.

Returning from exile in 1900, Lenin spent most of the next seventeen years in various European cities, reading, writing, plotting, and forming a series of shifting alliances with other socialists. In 1902 he published *What Is to Be Done?*, a political tract rejecting Marx's idea that workers would one day rise up on their own. Instead Lenin insisted that professional revolutionaries like himself—well organized, disciplined, and ruthless—were needed to spark the workers' revolt. At a socialist congress in 1903, Lenin managed to secure a temporary plurality of followers, who became known as Bolsheviks, which means "majority." His opponents—the Mensheviks, or "minority"—would suffer the bitterest scorn from Lenin's mouth and pen for their supposed timidity as revolutionists.

Lenin's hopes for widespread rebellion were partly realized in the 1905 Russian Revolution. On January 22 of that year, a Russian Orthodox priest led a peaceful protest of more than 150,000 people through the snowy streets of Saint Petersburg. The protesters carried a petition asking the czar to improve conditions for workers. When the crowd approached the czar's Winter Palace, soldiers suddenly opened fire, killing at least several hundred. Reports about Bloody Sunday, as it was called, quickly led to strikes and demonstrations throughout the country. In response, Czar Nicholas II offered some reforms, including limited civil rights and a legislative assembly. Nevertheless, further change was forestalled when troops returning from the failed Russo-Japanese War took to the streets to restore order. Intellectuals who had helped the workers organize, including Leon Trotsky, were arrested. Lenin, arriving in Saint Petersburg in December when the revolt was breaking up, avoided arrest and escaped first to Finland, then to Western Europe. He denounced the czar's empty promises and redoubled his efforts to organize and fund a revolutionary party.

The October Revolution

When World War I erupted in 1914, Lenin perceived the opportunity it presented. He hoped to turn the war between nations into a war between class enemies. Despite some setbacks—when Bolsheviks in the Russian parliament voted against war funding, they were arrested and exiled—war weariness eventually increased the people's readiness for change. As

Russian military defeats mounted and troops threatened to mutiny, support for Nicholas and his government collapsed. Nicholas, indecisive as a leader and alarmed at looming chaos in the streets, stepped down at the urging of a group of generals. Members of the moderate Socialist Revolutionary Party, led by Alexander Kerensky, set up what they called the Provisional Government to replace the czarist regime. At the same time, workers organized into soviets (workers' councils) to ensure that the new government did not favor the wealthy bourgeois interests. Thus, it was the February Revolution of 1917 (actually staged in March, according to the new-style calendar) that toppled the czar and shifted genuine power to a representative assembly.

Miles away in Switzerland, Lenin recognized the sway of events. Hurrying to Petrograd (the renamed Saint Petersburg), he railed against the new "bourgeois" government and called for its overthrow. The Provisional Government responded by arresting Lenin and his associate, the fiery revolutionary Leon Trotsky. While Trotsky was sent into Siberian exile,

Communists storm the old world of exploitation and inequality in a poster marking the anniversary of the 1917 October Revolution. The revolution, led by Vladimir Lenin and the Bolsheviks, ushered in the first modern totalitarian regime.

Lenin managed to escape to Finland again. He knew that the Provisional Government had little hope of succeeding in such a chaotic situation. Furthermore, Lenin's Bolsheviks, despite their small numbers, were the only opposition group that was well organized and ready to seize control. In late summer, when the provisional leader Kerensky accused the army's main general of planning a coup, he fumbled away the military's crucial support. Lenin saw the opportunity for which he had waited a lifetime. Convincing his followers that the time was ripe, Lenin and the Bolsheviks took control of the capital without a shot being fired. The takeover actually occurred on November 7, 1917 (or in October, according to the old-style calendar). To disguise his intentions, Lenin declared that the soviets would hold all power in a genuine democracy. Yet it was the Bolsheviks who were truly in charge, a position that would not be relinquished for more than seventy years.

> "Viewing the Bolsheviks' power seizure from the perspective of history, one can only marvel at their audacity."[6]
>
> —Richard Pipes, a historian.

Seizing power was one thing, but now Lenin and his followers had to govern. "Viewing the Bolsheviks' power seizure from the perspective of history," wrote historian Richard Pipes, "one can only marvel at their audacity. None of the leading Bolsheviks had experience in administering anything, and yet they were about to assume responsibility for governing the world's largest country. Nor, lacking business experience, did they shy from promptly nationalizing and hence assuming responsibility for managing the world's fifth-largest economy."[6] With loyal Bolsheviks making up only a tiny minority of the population and all other groups waiting for him to fail, Lenin had no choice but to rule as the czars always had: with the *silnaya ruka*, the iron fist of dictatorship. He was prepared to use any means necessary to maintain power and destroy his adversaries. For example (as indicated in Trotsky's diary), it was Lenin who ordered the murders of Nicholas II, his wife Alexandra, and their five children, a circumstance that Soviet historians officially denied until the 1990s. Spurred by fanaticism, Lenin's improvised dictatorship would soon become the first modern totalitarian regime.

Aftermath of the Revolution

In order to preserve the dictatorship, Lenin and the Bolsheviks first had to end Russia's involvement in World War I. Lenin agreed to an unpopular peace treaty with Germany, Austria, and other enemy nations that required Russia to relinquish large territories. The Bolsheviks also set about eliminating their opposition in a bloody civil war. The opposition, called the White Army, consisted of officers and soldiers who desperately sought to overthrow the Bolsheviks, some with the intention of restoring the czarist regime, some with notions of establishing a democratic government. Although they received little assistance from Western powers, the Whites managed to extend the civil war for three years. Ultimately, however, the Bolsheviks were victorious; their control of the large cities and factories gave them the advantages they needed to win. At the same time, the Bolsheviks, now calling themselves Communists, looked beyond Russia's borders to the idea of world revolution. Lenin and his associates were deadly serious with regard to Marx's slogan, "Workers of the world, unite!" Trotsky observed that expanding Soviet power required a sort of constant civil war. As events developed, Lenin and his followers conducted what amounted to a hostile occupation of their own country.

Immediately after the revolution, Lenin feigned his support for democracy by authorizing long-delayed elections to the Constituent Assembly. When rival parties won twice the number of votes than the Bolsheviks, Lenin claimed the election did not represent the true wishes of the workers and soldiers and dissolved the assembly after its first day. In its place he created the Council of People's Commissars, made up entirely of Bolsheviks. (A commissar was a Communist Party official who enforced party principles and loyalty.) To further cement Communist rule, he did away with the legal system, replacing formal trials with Revolutionary Tribunals headed by party supporters. Lenin also decreed the end of private property, allowing peasants to seize control of farmlands and estates that had previously belonged to their landlords. Workers were encouraged to take charge of factories. These moves actually were temporary measures intended to placate the people until the new Communist government was sufficiently powerful to assume full control.

The Russian Revolution Through Western Eyes

News reports of the czar's overthrow in 1917 drew plenty of excited commentary in the West. Officially, the US government opposed the Bolsheviks and joined with allies in support of the White Army during the civil war. The US Department of Justice responded to domestic fears about Bolshevism in America by investigating trade union leaders and other suspected revolutionaries. Attorney General A. Mitchell Palmer selected J. Edgar Hoover to conduct inquiries that led to the Palmer Raids, in which suspected foreign radicals in several cities were arrested and questioned. It was probably the most hostile environment for Soviet communism until the Red Scare and the McCarthy hearings in the 1950s. (This was an episode in which Senator Joseph McCarthy led a congressional inquiry into Communist infiltration in American government and society.) The US government did not officially recognize the Soviet Union diplomatically until 1933 under President Franklin D. Roosevelt. Nevertheless, many intellectuals in the West viewed the events in Russia as a great triumph for human freedom and were not shy about saying so. Lincoln Steffens, an American muckraking journalist and activist, visited Soviet Russia in 1919 and famously remarked, "I have seen the future and it works." The Irish playwright George Bernard Shaw visited four times between 1926 and 1931, heaping praise on what he considered a great societal transformation. Legend has it that Lenin referred to these enthusiastic defenders of the Soviet Union as "useful idiots." Soviet officials doubtless saw value in any endorsements from Western visitors and were quick to use them for propaganda.

Quoted in Kevin Baker, "Lincoln Steffens: Muckraker's Progress." *New York Times*, May 13, 2011. www.nytimes.com.

To carry out the government's wide-ranging schemes required an enormous bureaucracy of loyal functionaries, a development that Lenin disliked but found necessary. Instead of the state withering away under communism, as predicted in Marx's writings, it became larger and more convoluted than it had been under the czar. Communist officials with special ties to Josef Stalin, a member of Lenin's trusted inner circle, became part of a group called the *nomenklatura*. Their loyalty won them privileges, such as vacations at southern resorts, special food and medical care, and more spacious living quarters. Stalin found this network of loyalists invaluable to his rise within the Communist Party. Perhaps most ominous of all the new arrangements was Lenin's creation of the Cheka, a ruthless secret police force dedicated to rooting out enemies of the new regime. With remarkable speed Lenin and his followers sketched the blueprint for the future of the Soviet Union.

> "Comrade Stalin, having become secretary-general, has boundless power concentrated in his hands, and I am not sure whether he will always be capable of using that power with sufficient caution."[7]
>
> —Soviet leader Vladimir Lenin.

Lenin's Successor

Lenin himself would not live to see much more of Soviet Russia's future. In failing health ever since being wounded in a 1918 assassination attempt, Lenin suffered a stroke in May 1921 and gradually was forced to give up his political work. Before his death in 1924, Lenin recorded his thoughts about his fellow revolutionaries, including Stalin, who succeeded Lenin as head of the party. "Comrade Stalin," wrote Lenin, "having become secretary-general, has boundless power concentrated in his hands, and I am not sure whether he will always be capable of using that power with sufficient caution."[7] This from a man who thought nothing of using terror as state policy or employing "famine relief" as a pretext for confiscating church property worth hundreds of millions of rubles (the Russian currency). Yet events would show that Lenin was justified in his wariness about Stalin.

CHAPTER TWO

A Tradition of Tyranny

The political goal for Lenin and subsequently for Stalin and other Soviet leaders was always simple: Communist Party rule must be preserved at all costs. Rival parties and factions were not allowed. Opinions that diverged from the Bolshevik line drew swift reprisal. The Bolsheviks considered themselves a paramilitary group in the midst of a populace that could not be trusted and must be conditioned by force to the new reality. Like Lenin after the October Revolution, Stalin quickly demonstrated his willingness to use violence and terror against anyone who opposed the party's objectives.

The Beginning of Stalinism

After Lenin's death in 1924, the task of maintaining the party's dominance fell to a troika (or trio) of officials that included Josef Stalin. Born Josef Djugashvili in the Russian state of Georgia, Stalin (the name was derived from the Russian word for "steel") was not well educated but possessed the wiles of a seasoned conspirator. While Lenin was still alive, Stalin had plotted with other Bolsheviks to blacken the name of Leon Trotsky, his main rival for power, and eventually succeeded in getting Trotsky exiled. Stalin soon managed to push aside his associates in the troika, eliminate challengers from both the left wing and right wing of the party, and assume control of the party and government as supreme leader. Once in control, he saw to it that politics in the ordinary sense ceased to exist in the Soviet Union.

Stalin immediately set the country on a more radical course. Rapid industrialization and collectivization of agriculture were forced on the populace. In collectivization, peasant farms were forcibly joined together in an attempt to improve their efficiency. To ensure cooperation at every level, Stalin created an atmosphere of continual crisis. The regime required people to make huge sacrifices for the cause of communism: working long hours for little pay, living in tiny communal apartments, subsisting on small rations of food. Those who complained or failed to follow party directives faced retribution from the vast bureaucracy or the secret police.

In the 1930s, with the Soviet Union having achieved a measure of success in its economic goals, the highest party officials contemplated a change in leadership. They believed Stalin to be too militant to govern during quieter periods. Several of the officials proposed that Sergei Kirov, a loyal Stalinist and rising star in the party, should become general secretary. When Stalin learned of the plan, his murderous instincts took over. Here was a chance to manufacture a new crisis and spread fear within both the government and the citizenry. In December 1934 Kirov fell to an assassin's bullets. "At Kirov's funeral," wrote Robert Conquest, an expert on the Stalinist period, "Stalin bent and kissed the cheeks of the corpse, who was certainly more useful to him dead than alive. For the assassination was the key moment in Stalin's drive to total power."[8]

> "At Kirov's funeral, Stalin bent and kissed the cheeks of the corpse, who was certainly more useful to him dead than alive. For the assassination was the key moment in Stalin's drive to total power."[8]
>
> —Robert Conquest, a historian and an expert on the Stalinist period.

The Great Terror

Kirov's murder enabled Stalin to claim that "enemies of the people" were everywhere. The Communist regime was under attack by all sorts of spies and counterrevolutionaries. Kirov's assassin was arrested and shot, along with several members of his family—a fiendish Stalinist touch that would only grow more frequent. As Stalin's orchestrated paranoia grew, the Great Terror began, and arrests outpaced the ability of tribunals to keep up. Suspects by the thousands were tried, convicted of treason, and either shot or delivered to prison camps. Informers appeared, bent on showing their loyalty to the regime by ratting on their neighbors. One Soviet boy was hailed as a patriotic hero for informing on his father. No one was safe from the violence, from rank and file party members to generals in the Red Army to cultural figures like the theatrical producer Vsevolod Meyerhold. Secret archives uncovered after the fall of the Soviet Union showed that at the height of the Terror—1937 and 1938—more than 1.5 million citizens were arrested for un-Soviet activities, of which almost 700,000 were shot. Those who survived ended up in labor camps. Bureaucratic lists of quotas have been discovered, detailing the number of victims required in different regions. Even party membership offered no protection: of 1,966 delegates to the 1934 Communist Party Congress, 1,108 were eventually seized and convicted.

Among the victims of the Great Terror were the Old Bolsheviks who had helped engineer the October Revolution. Their public trials excited

Opponents of the Soviet regime were locked away, sometimes for decades, in isolated prison camps, such as Perm 35 (pictured in 1989, shortly after the first foreign journalists were allowed into the site). Under Stalin's Great Terror, thousands were tried, convicted, and imprisoned in camps like this one.

The Gulag

The Gulag was the system of forced labor camps that grew tremendously as Stalin pursued his policies of rapid industrialization and collectivized farming. The term *Gulag* is an acronym for the bureaucratic group that ran the system, but it also symbolizes much more. According to Anne Applebaum, an expert on the Soviet camps, "'Gulag' has come to mean the Soviet repressive system itself, the set of procedures that prisoners once called the 'meat-grinder': the arrests, the interrogations, the transport in unheated cattle cars, the forced labor, the destruction of families, the years spent in exile, the early and unnecessary deaths."

At its height, the Gulag held more than 2 million prisoners. The largest camps lay far to the Arctic north and the Siberian northeast. Many prisoners were ordinary citizens who had somehow fallen afoul of Soviet policies or Stalinist paranoia. Following arrest and sentencing with no recourse to a trial, an individual faced years of imprisonment and hard labor in conditions that were almost beyond human endurance. Death rates in the camps soared due to extreme cold, meager rations, backbreaking labor, and cramped and unsanitary living conditions.

In 1973 the writer and former prisoner Aleksandr Solzhenitsyn published *The Gulag Archipelago*, a work that made the Gulag notorious the world over. In the book, Solzhenitsyn described his own arrest and imprisonment alongside similar stories he had gathered from hundreds of other inmates. While the Gulag diminished some after Stalin's death in 1953, it continued to hold political prisoners up to the Soviet Union's collapse.

Anne Applebaum, *Gulag: A History.* New York: Anchor, 2004, pp. xv–xvi.

keen interest in the West. Observers were puzzled at how these former heroes of the revolution—men like Grigory Zinoviev, Lev Kamenev, and Nikolai Bukharin—could become traitors against the regime they helped to build. Having been broken by torture, the Old Bolsheviks and other high officials confessed to false accusations in open court. These staged "show trials" designed for Western consumption demonstrated the lengths to which Stalin would go to strengthen his grip on power. In 1940, as a sort of epilogue to the purges, a Stalinist agent in Mexico murdered the exiled Trotsky with an ice pick blow to his head. By the beginning of World War II, Stalin stood unchallenged as Soviet leader. He had become for the Russian people an infallible, godlike figure. This state of affairs, known as a cult of personality, has been a noted feature of many other Communist dictatorships.

World War II and the Soviet Bloc

Stalin's reputation for infallibility among Communist sympathizers in the West was tested when he signed a nonaggression pact with Adolf Hitler and Nazi Germany in 1939. Almost all of Stalin's supporters endorsed the move as necessary to safeguard the Communist state. Politically, Stalin was always prepared to take whatever actions were most likely to benefit the Soviet Union, regardless of previous statements or positions. Soon Hitler reneged on the agreement and invaded Russia in June 1941. The Red Army found itself in a perilous situation. The Great Terror had done away with many of its most experienced officers, leaving Soviet troops to be managed by amateurs. As Conquest remarked, "Not only was there a disastrous shortage of trained officers at every level as a result of Stalin's purge of the army, but the purge and its 'vigilance' had made the remaining commanders timid and ruined their sense of initiative."[9] The result was staggering losses among Soviet troops. Scholars estimate that some 8.7 million Russian soldiers were killed in combat during World War II.

Yet the Red Army's resilience coupled with the endless snows of Russia enabled the Soviet Union to defeat the Germans. To mobilize the war effort, Stalin encouraged feelings of national pride among the people, urging them to defend the Motherland and referring to the war effort as the Great Patriotic War. For the first time in the Bolshevik era, ordinary Russians overwhelmingly supported their government. The Soviet victory paid immediate dividends. At war's end in 1945, Stalin ordered his troops to occupy most of Eastern and Central Europe, where they installed Communist regimes answerable to the Kremlin. Formerly an isolated Communist state, the Soviet Union had now become a large political bloc, with satellite states to do its bidding. In 1946 the

Soviet Union also took its place on the Security Council of the new United Nations, where it could effectively veto Western initiatives against it. With Mao Zedong's successful revolution in China, the world seemed destined for Communist domination. Fearing the worst, Great Britain's wartime prime minister, Winston Churchill, warned in a speech that an "iron curtain" had descended across Eastern Europe and that the Soviet Union was bent on expansion. The speech ushered in the Cold War, an ideological battle between Soviet communism and the democratic West. When the Soviet regime obtained its own atomic bomb in 1949, a prolonged military stalemate began. The United States led the West in promoting a policy of containment, with the idea of preventing the spread of communism.

Khrushchev's Secret Speech

Stalin's last months were focused less on Communist expansion than on his campaign to crush Jewish dissidents in the Soviet Union. His death in 1953 brought to power a collective leadership from which Nikita Khrushchev emerged as the main figure. Khrushchev and other Soviet officials recognized that Stalin's policies had to be repudiated. The question was how to do this while still insisting that the Communist regime was sound and deserving of the *nomenklatura*'s support. Khrushchev's solution was to make a secret speech to the Twentieth Congress of the Communist Party in 1956. In the speech, he acknowledged some of Stalin's crimes and hearkened back to Lenin as the true guiding spirit of communism. At once Stalin's corpse vanished from Lenin's mausoleum in Red Square, the city of Stalingrad became Volgograd, and the countless images of Stalin throughout the nation disappeared. However, despite his bloody legacy, the dictator remained popular among many ordinary Russians. As Danish journalist Samuel Rachlin wrote, "The fact is that the de-Stalinization campaign was never completed, either by Nikita Khrushchev or his successors. Under Leonid Brezhnev's long rule, Stalin was relegated to a no man's land of history that allowed a half-hidden cult to persist in a mixture of defiance and protest against the weakness of the Kremlin rulers."[10]

While the new Soviet leadership may have seemed weak compared to Stalin, it was still more than capable of taking swift and brutal action.

Soviet tanks roll into the Hungarian capital of Budapest in 1956. The Soviets sought to crush an anticommunist revolt—and in the process killed as many as thirty thousand protesters.

Hopes among dissidents for a new post-Stalinist era of political openness and freedom soon came crashing down. The same year of Khrushchev's secret speech saw Red Army tanks roll into Budapest, the capital of Hungary, to quell an uprising among students and workers seeking an end to Soviet control. Invading forces killed as many as thirty thousand protesters—dubbed "hooligans" by *Pravda*, a Soviet newspaper. More than a decade later, an attempt at liberalization in Czechoslovakia brought a similar Soviet response. In both cases the Soviet leadership justified its intervention as necessary to protect Communist governments. This policy was known as the Brezhnev Doctrine, after Leonid Brezhnev, the hard-line general secretary who succeeded Khrushchev. The United States and other Western countries denounced these invasions, but ultimately they decided to live with Soviet actions that only defended established territory and did not seek to expand its empire. Indeed, the 1970s became an era of détente between the Soviet Union and the West—a generally peaceful time of limited engagement.

Gorbachev's Reforms

During the period of détente, Brezhnev and the Politburo (the policy-making body in the Soviet Union) emphasized economic control and military growth. This led to a general stagnation that by the 1980s could no longer be ignored. Corruption and disillusionment riddled the empire. Vibrant dissident voices were gaining authority. By contrast, Brezhnev, who died in 1982, and his successors were old men with tired ideas. Thus, in 1985 the deeply conservative Politburo resolved to take a different tack and chose Mikhail Gorbachev to lead the Communist Party. At age fifty-four, Gorbachev projected a new image of health and vitality to the nation. Despite his repeated claims to be a staunch Marxist-Leninist, he soon began to demonstrate a commitment to real change, including a general policy of *perestroika*, or restructuring, of Soviet government and society. Proposals for market reforms, increased economic activity by individuals, multicandidate elections, and appointment of nonparty members to government posts were just some of the new ideas.

The most seismic of Gorbachev's reforms was *glasnost*, or openness. Like Khrushchev, Gorbachev was willing to acknowledge Stalin's crimes, but this time it was done in a speech broadcast to the entire nation. In addition, Gorbachev allowed the publication of previously outlawed books, such as Boris Pasternak's *Doctor Zhivago*, with its critical look at the October Revolution; and Aleksandr Solzhenitsyn's *The Gulag Archipelago*, about the horrors of the Soviet prison camp system. Yet Gorbachev went further than merely allowing an honest look at the Soviet past. BBC Moscow correspondent Martin Sixsmith wrote:

> More problematical were issues of current politics. In previous times, the Communist monopoly on information meant that difficult facts, problems with industrial or agricultural production, news of disasters, failures, political discontent or state crimes and corruption,

would never find their way into the public domain. Information about the successes of the West was concealed by a ban on foreign publications and the jamming of the BBC Russian Service, the US Radio Liberty and the Voice of America. After a period of initial hesitation, Gorbachev began to relax many of those restrictions.[11]

An example of glasnost in action came in April 1986. The nuclear reactor at Chernobyl in Ukraine exploded, sending radiation three hundred times normal levels shooting into the atmosphere. After the Soviet government initially denied the accident and accused Western media of spreading lies, Gorbachev went on Russian television and admitted the facts—an enormous break with past habits of Soviet propaganda. This new openness won him admiration in the West, where he was twice named *Time* magazine's Man of the Year. In 1988 Gorbachev authorized elections to the Congress of People's Deputies, giving Soviet citizens a chance to choose their representatives for the first time since 1917. The elections brought many non-Communists and liberal reformers to office, including Boris Yeltsin, the Moscow party chief who would soon become Gorbachev's chief rival.

The Collapse of the Soviet Union

In setting these changes into motion, Gorbachev failed to realize how explosive they would be. With the freedom to criticize the government came bitter impatience when the pace of change did not match expectations. At the same time, a countermovement of old-guard conservatives arose within the government. These party members, some of them open Stalinists, opposed Gorbachev's

> "In previous times, the Communist monopoly on information meant that difficult facts, problems with industrial or agricultural production, news of disasters, failures, political discontent or state crimes and corruption, would never find their way into the public domain. . . . After a period of initial hesitation, Gorbachev began to relax many of those restrictions."[11]
>
> —Martin Sixsmith, a BBC Moscow correspondent.

Andrei Sakharov and the Dissident Movement

Dissidents in the Soviet Union were those who spoke out openly against government repression and advocated for political freedom. The dissidents' protests, which inevitably led to their censorship or even arrest, nevertheless showed that the Soviet Union was far from the harmonious society it claimed to be. One of the most influential dissidents was Andrei Sakharov (1921–1989), a leading nuclear physicist. In 1961 Sakharov angered Soviet officials by pointing out the dangers of radioactive fallout in Khrushchev's plan for an atmospheric nuclear test. The incident led Sakharov to focus on political matters. His 1968 essay called for reductions in nuclear arms and criticized the treatment of Soviet dissidents. Editors refused to publish the piece, but like many important dissident writings it was circulated in typewritten copies called *samizdat*. In 1975 Sakharov received the Nobel Peace Prize for his commitment to principles of peace and his opposition to the abuse of power. When the Soviet government prevented him from accepting the award in person, Sakharov sent his wife, Yelena Bonner, in his place. In 1980 Sakharov denounced the Soviet invasion of Afghanistan, which resulted in his exile to the city of Gorky in western Russia. Four years later his wife was also exiled to Gorky for her own anti-Soviet political activity. In 1986, following Sakharov's months-long hunger strike that made headlines in the West, Gorbachev released the scientist and his wife and allowed them to live in Moscow. Widely celebrated for his courage, Sakharov lived to see Gorbachev institute many of the reforms he had long demanded.

reforms, fearing that they would lead to chaos and ultimate collapse. In November 1989 came the fall of the Berlin Wall, the barrier separating Communist East Germany from the West. When Gorbachev and the Politburo declined to intervene, it was obvious that the Soviet system was tottering.

Soon Gorbachev and his fellow reformers fell victim to the tidal wave of change they had unleashed. Independence movements broke out among the Baltic states of Lithuania, Latvia, and Estonia, with similar movements arising in Ukraine, Georgia, and other areas of central Asia. As Gorbachev grew more embattled, Yeltsin's fortunes continued to rise. In June 1991 Yeltsin won the presidency of the newly independent Russian Federation. Two months later hard-line Communists, alarmed at the rising calls for independence among the republics, launched a last-ditch putsch (or coup attempt) to preserve the Soviet Union. They imprisoned Gorbachev in his Crimean vacation home and removed him from power. However, the hard-liners' attempt at a takeover failed due to lack of support among the people and the deeply divided military and KGB (the Soviet secret police and spy agency). "The conspirators had launched the putsch to save the Soviet empire and their positions in it," observed David Remnick, a correspondent on the scene for the *Washington Post*. "Their failure was the finishing blow. No Baltic independence movement, no Russian liberals, had ever done as much to bring it all down."[12] Yeltsin, who took to the streets to rally opposition to the coup, emerged as a national hero. One of his first acts after the coup attempt was to ban the Communist Party. Thus, in a dizzying rush of events, the Soviet Union came to an end.

Yeltsin Gives Way to Putin

At first Yeltsin seemed capable of rising above the chaotic developments in Russia. A referendum election in 1993 showed strong support for his efforts to establish democracy and free markets. Yet Yeltsin's headlong approach to revamping the economy and privatizing commercial interests amounted to shock therapy. While some grew fantastically wealthy, conditions among most Russians soon began to deteriorate. The economy faltered, and food shortages threatened to spur a revolt. In a clash with conservatives who were threatening civil war, Yeltsin ordered troops to shell the parliament building. He also sent forces to put down a rebellion in the republic of Chechnya, which led to a lingering and unpopular war. Beset by these difficulties as well as serious health

Vladimir Putin speaks at a 2012 presidential campaign rally. When Putin originally took over the presidency from Boris Yeltsin in 1999 he reversed the democratic reforms of his predecessors and orchestrated a return to authoritarian government.

problems, Yeltsin finally resigned the presidency in 1999, handing power to Vladimir Putin, a former KGB officer whom Yeltsin trusted to continue his program of reforms.

Instead of reforms, Putin engineered a return to authoritarian government. He embarked on a course he called managed democracy, which amounted to a pushback against democratic reforms and individual freedom. He insisted that the Western-style democracy favored by Yeltsin was not suitable for Russia and inevitably led to chaos. "For Russians," Putin said, "a strong state is not an anomaly to be got rid of. Quite the contrary, they see it as a source and guarantor of order."[13]

Putin proved masterful at consolidating power by controlling the media and intimidating his enemies, such as the tycoons who had benefited from privatization. When faced with constitutional limits on a third consecutive term as president, Putin simply installed an associate and continued to rule as prime minister. His swaggering appearance on the world stage appealed to Russians who regretted their nation's loss of prestige in the 1990s. While not comparable to Stalin's mystique, Putin's own cult of personality continued to grow. To many observers, Putin was simply the latest in a long line of Russian tyrants, a line that extended from the czars to the Soviets to the present day.

> "For Russians, a strong state is not an anomaly to be got rid of. Quite the contrary, they see it as a source and guarantor of order."[13]
>
> —Russian Federation president Vladimir Putin.

CHAPTER THREE

From Communism to Free Markets

In his state of the nation speech in December 2013, Russian president Vladimir Putin admitted that Russia's economic problems were not due to Europe's debt crisis but rather were self-inflicted. The remarkable growth from rising oil prices that had marked Putin's first two terms in office had begun to subside. While the lot of ordinary Russians had improved, the global recession of 2008 had hit Russia particularly hard. Now economists were predicting nothing but stagnation going forward. Many experts blamed Putin's policies for the cronyism and corruption that marked the decline. Despite the success of economic reforms in his earlier years in office, Putin had reverted to threats and bullying tactics in his dealings with corporate owners. His efforts to diversify Russia's economy had mostly failed. In a September 19, 2013, *Pravda* editorial addressed to the Russian people, US senator John McCain wrote, "[Putin] has given you an economy that is based almost entirely on a few natural resources that will rise and fall with those commodities. Its riches will not last. And, while they do, they will be mostly in the possession of the corrupt and powerful few."[14] Russia's economy in the twenty-first century, much like in the days of the czars and the Soviets, saw the nation's wealth concentrated in the hands of favored individuals while the vast majority struggled to better themselves.

War Communism

Russia's wealth had been depleted by war when Lenin and the Bolsheviks seized control in 1917. At the beginning the Bolshevik regime was fragile, with most of its support confined to the cities. Everyday economic life had ground to a halt as workers and civil servants, their wages unpaid, went on strike against the Bolshevik takeover. Having negotiated an end to Russia's involvement in World War I, Lenin and the Bolsheviks turned their attention to winning the civil war with the White Army. To accomplish this goal, the Bolsheviks adopted a socialist program of emergency measures called War Communism. Lenin decreed an end to private property and allowed land holdings to be divided among the peasantry, a move that helped secure the peasants' loyalty—or at least bought off their hostility. At the same time, workers were encouraged to take over factories, banks, shipping, and other industries. Capitalism was outlawed, and the state seized all businesses with more than ten employees. A food commissariat carried out the distribution of food, with manual laborers receiving preference over the professional classes. These

Workers drill for oil in western Siberia. During Vladimir Putin's first two terms as president, rising oil prices promoted steady growth in Russia, but the country's economy has suffered since the 2008 global recession.

policies convinced many workers and peasants to join the Red Army and fight the counterrevolutionary Whites, who were certain to return any seized property to its previous owners.

Despite the workers' general support, War Communism proved disastrous. None of the new leaders were serious economists or managers, and they governed by ideology, not practical experience. For example, money was virtually abolished and the ruble plummeted in value because the Bolsheviks preferred a barter economy, in which goods were exchanged without the use of currency. Peasants on outlying farms began to grow only enough food for themselves, knowing that any extra would be taken by the state's requisition squads. This practice left cities with dangerous shortages of food. Malnutrition and disease spread throughout the nation. Weary workers, many assigned to unfamiliar new tasks, failed to keep the factories running efficiently. Foreign trade was nonexistent, since other nations refused to deal with the Communists. Nevertheless, the Bolsheviks managed to preserve most workers' loyalty by blaming shortages on the war and the White Army. Lenin gave orders to arrest anyone who complained. His early use of terror to intimidate the populace included random executions of those labeled as enemies. Perhaps the most valuable aspect of War Communism to the Bolsheviks was the way it allowed them to consolidate their power more rapidly.

The harsh policies of War Communism coincided with—indeed helped bring about—a deadly famine throughout Russia. Drought conditions in grain-producing areas made things even worse. Peasant uprisings broke out in protest against the Bolsheviks' requisitioning of grain. By 1921 the United States, at the Soviets' request, was distributing food in a massive relief effort. Overall, about one-tenth of the population perished in the early years of the revolution.

The New Economic Policy

Faced with mass starvation and peasant rebellions, Lenin and his associates abandoned War Communism in favor of a radically different approach. The New Economic Policy (NEP), adopted by the Tenth Congress of the Communist Party in March 1921, reinstated a market economy through a moderate tax on food crops. In essence, by taxing food instead of seizing it by force, the Communists were admitting that people owned their stores of grain. Peasant farmers were now allowed to sell their excess grain in the cities, which gave them incentive to produce at a higher level.

All this flew in the face of Lenin's Marxist ideals but enabled the Bolsheviks to maintain power. The Communists' initial experiment with a planned economy had nearly broken the country. The NEP, by contrast, led to rapid expansion in agricultural production and light industry. Lenin acknowledged that War Communism had been too bitter a medicine and rationalized the NEP as a necessary intermediate step to full-scale socialism, in which all economic decisions would come from the central government.

One valuable aspect of the NEP was its short-term solution of the peasant problem. With greater economic freedom, the peasants ceased to revolt and concentrated on farming and taking newly available jobs in logging and construction. Nevertheless, Lenin continued to view the Russian peasant as the enemy of the revolution. For the Communists, the peasants' desire to improve their lot on their own had to be bent to the will of the state. The lengths to which the Communists would go is indicated in a 1918 speech by one of the original Bolsheviks, Grigory Zinoviev: "We must carry along with us 90 million out of the 100 million Soviet Russian population. As for the rest, we have nothing to say to them. They must be annihilated."[15]

It was just such revolutionary fervor that inspired the Bolsheviks' plans to create the ideal Communist state. After Lenin's death, the Soviet government resumed its relentless push to reorganize Russian society. The Communist Party Congress of 1925 resolved to pursue an ambitious plan of forced industrialization, which called for increased agricultural production as well. By 1927 the NEP had expanded economic activity in Russia almost to prewar levels. Yet Stalin and his supporters in the party's inner circle regretted

> "We must carry along with us 90 million out of the 100 million Soviet Russian population. As for the rest, we have nothing to say to them. They must be annihilated."[15]
>
> —Grigory Zinoviev, a member of the Bolshevik inner circle.

what they saw as a revival of capitalism and its ills, including exploitation of workers, stubborn unemployment, and a return of bourgeois values. In response, Stalin prepared to abandon the market economy and bring back socialism with a vengeance.

Collectivization and the War Against the Kulaks

To reinstate true socialism and solve the problem of food shortages, especially among industrial workers in the cities, Stalin announced his Five-Year Plan to collectivize agriculture in the Soviet Union. This meant organizing peasant farmlands into huge collectives that could be run like factories or large businesses. It was thought that this new organization would lead to more efficient production and much higher yields of grain than had been possible with the peasants' strip-farming methods. Another aim of the new policy was to eliminate a class of peasants called kulaks. According to party propaganda, kulaks were enemies of the people—wealthy peasants who loaned money to their neighbors at onerous interest rates. In Communist pamphlets they were often called "bloodsuckers" and "exploiters." In practice, however, most kulaks were successful small landholders who had managed, with discipline and persistence, to accrue some wealth, generally in farmland and livestock. As community leaders in the countryside, kulaks represented a counterweight to Soviet power. Thus, by Stalinist logic they had to be crushed. "What does this mean?" wrote Stalin in 1929. "It means that we have passed from the policy of *restricting* the exploiting proclivities of the kulaks to the policy of *eliminating* the kulaks as a class."[16]

> "What does this mean? It means that we have passed from the policy of *restricting* the exploiting proclivities of the kulaks to the policy of *eliminating* the kulaks as a class."[16]
>
> —Josef Stalin, general secretary of the Communist Party.

Elimination of the kulaks proceeded in tandem with collectivization. Regional party officials and activists from the cities descended on the villages to convince skeptical peasants to enroll in collectivization. Those

Gun-wielding Bolsheviks demonstrate their power in 1920. The emergency measures undertaken by Lenin around this time included government seizure of private property and assignment of workers to unfamiliar jobs.

who balked could be labeled as kulaks and threatened with confiscation of their property. Some peasants sold out immediately. Most, however, hesitated. In 1930 Stalin doubled down on the policy and on the harassment of the kulaks. Brigades of party activists poured into the most important grain-producing regions like an invading army. They sought to break down kulak resistance and persuade the peasantry to do their patriotic duty. Peasants labeled as kulaks had their land and property seized. They were then resettled nearby, deported, imprisoned in labor camps, or shot. Anyone caught giving aid to evicted kulaks was also subject to arrest. The intimidation proved effective. By July 1932 more than 60 percent of peasant households had joined collective farms.

The peasants on collective farms were little more than slave laborers who worked long hours for subsistence wages. Yet Stalin had further plans to eliminate the peasantry as a political nuisance to the Soviet state. In July 1932 the party decreed that all property on collective farms,

The Terror Famine

The worst of Stalin's murderous famine occurred in Ukraine and North Caucasus. Ukraine was a fertile region known as the breadbasket of Europe, with its own language and proud cultural traditions. It had long sought independence from Moscow, even in czarist times, and thus drew Stalin's special attention. When rural Ukrainians rebelled against Stalin's collectivist policies, Red Army troops and secret police rushed in to restore order. Many peasants continued to resist, leaving crops to rot in unharvested fields. Stalin's response was to seize all available grain (actually a sizable harvest in 1932) for sale on the foreign market and to let the Ukrainians starve. Soviet troops sealed the borders, turning the region into a huge concentration camp. "In the terrible spring of 1933," recalled a Soviet activist, "I saw people dying from hunger. I saw women and children with distended bellies, turning blue, still breathing but with vacant, lifeless eyes. And corpses—corpses in ragged sheepskin coats and cheap felt boots; corpses in peasant huts, in the melting snow of the old Vologda, under the bridges of Kharkov."

Reports of the Ukrainian famine reached the West, but nothing was said or done. Many newspapers followed the Soviet line that the famine never happened. Having achieved his goals of eliminating the kulaks as a class and curtailing the independence of village farmers, Stalin relented and allowed food to be distributed inside Ukraine. His terror famine had caused as many as 7 million deaths, including 3 million children.

Quoted in Robert Conquest, *The Harvest of Sorrow: Soviet Collectivization and the Terror-Famine.* New York: Oxford University Press, 1986, p. 233.

including cattle, grain, and other produce, belonged to the state. Any peasants reserving it for their own use were to be summarily shot, unless there were special circumstances, in which case they were to be arrested and sent to a prison camp. At the same time, the state set unreasonable quotas for grain requisition. Every available ounce of grain was subject to confiscation for state use. Peasants were essentially forbidden to eat the food they harvested. The result was a deliberately created famine on an almost unimaginable scale.

Industrialization and the Postwar Economy

While famine raged in the countryside, Stalin's program of rapid industrialization in the cities was a rousing success. No country in history had ever expanded its industrial base so rapidly. By the end of the second Five-Year Plan in 1938, Soviet production of steel and coal had more than tripled. The Soviet Union led the world in making railway cars and farm tractors. One reason for Stalin's focus on industrialization was his belief that another world war was inevitable and that the nation must be prepared to take advantage of it. Nevertheless, in 1941 when Nazi Germany broke its nonaggression pact with the Soviet Union and attacked eastward, the Red Army was initially overwhelmed. Only a valiant last-ditch nine-hundred-day stand at Leningrad (what is today once again Saint Petersburg) enabled the Soviets to defeat Hitler's troops. Despite his crimes against the Russian people, Stalin was hailed as a shrewd military leader and his country's savior.

The Soviet Union's postwar economy rebounded rapidly even while its government remained rigidly centralized. In the 1950s and 1960s, the Soviets responded to the challenges of the Cold War by spending vast amounts on the military and the support of Communist movements in the Third World. Soviet leaders saw nuclear weapons as a great equalizer and spent massive amounts of money developing them. The breakthrough missile technology represented by the launch of the *Sputnik* satellite in 1957 gave the impression that the Soviet Union was capable of outpacing the West both militarily and economically. In reality, however, the Soviet economy was plagued by shortages, poor-quality consumer goods, and diversion of too many resources to the military—by some estimates, as much as 40 percent of national income. Widespread corruption also hamstrung economic activity. Bribery, kickbacks, and theft of state property were shrugged off as facts of everyday life. The 1970s saw the Soviet economy stagnate to levels below that of most Western industrial nations and even some eastern European countries. Shortages led workers to carry net bags with them at all times in case they heard about a nearby store receiving a shipment of food. One product that remained readily available was vodka. Alcoholism was a key factor in the decline in life expectancy during the Brezhnev years.

Gorbachev's Economic Reforms

In the late 1980s Mikhail Gorbachev's policy of perestroika sought to reverse more than two decades of economic stagnation. As a committed socialist, Gorbachev believed that the Soviet system was basically sound. Rather than remake the Soviet economy along the lines of the West's free markets, he hoped to introduce smaller modernizing adjustments. Workers were urged to be more productive through slogans posted in workplaces like "Intensification and Acceleration." He dealt with alcoholism by curbing the production of spirits (and inadvertently helped establish a thriving underground market for vodka). He shut down the most inefficient factories and allowed a limited number of private businesses to open. However, Gorbachev's reforms, while on the right track, were not extensive enough to be successful. His frequent boasts about the changes that were coming backfired when Soviet citizens continued to see empty shelves and long lines at retail shops. He was late in realizing that deeper structural changes were needed to revitalize the economy. By trying to steer a middle course between radical reformers and skeptical conservatives, Gorbachev ended up losing the people's support.

When Boris Yeltsin won the Russian presidency in 1991, he used his new platform to promote Russian nationalism and radical economic reform. Under Yeltsin, Russia began to function as an independent state. Many Russians came to believe that the Bolshevik revolution and the Soviet drive to create an empire were huge mistakes that had prevented Russia from following the historical path that led to western European–style prosperity. Yeltsin encouraged the Russian parliament to pass reforms to create a market economy. Following the failed coup attempt that hastened

In the late 1980s residents of Moscow line up outside a store that has shoes for sale. Mikhail Gobachev's economic reforms were not bold enough to fill empty store shelves or to end long lines at stores that had products to sell.

the fall of the Soviet Union, Yeltsin focused on transforming the Russian Federation into a capitalist country.

Economic Chaos in Post-Soviet Russia

Like many of the other former Soviet republics, the Russian Federation saw its new independence quickly turn to chaos. Mistakes made in Gorbachev's last years were compounded by Yeltsin's fumbling attempts to establish capitalism. Changing from a fully centralized economy to a market-based system brought many new problems. Price controls on most consumer goods, instituted by Gorbachev, led to even greater scarcity. The whole system of distributing goods threatened to collapse. When Yeltsin removed price controls in January 1992, inflation soared. The value of the ruble collapsed, wiping out many Russians' life savings.

Gazprom, One of the World's Most Powerful Companies

Much of Russia's economic history in the last fifty years is summarized in the fortunes of Gazprom, the huge natural gas company. Gazprom originated as the Soviet Gas Ministry in 1965. It represented the government's new focus on tapping Russia's enormous reserves of natural gas. In 1989, as part of Mikhail Gorbachev's reform program, the ministry became Gazprom, a state-owned company headed by former gas minister Viktor Chernomyrdin. In 1992, when Boris Yeltsin named Chernomyrdin to be Russia's prime minister, control of Gazprom passed to a tight group of associates. The corporation sold shares to private investors, who became fabulously wealthy. Unlike other Russian energy companies, which had to compete with each other, Gazprom remained a monopoly.

In 2005 Vladimir Putin reasserted government ownership of 51 percent of Gazprom. The company's president and its chair of the board are both close friends of Putin.

With control of 25 percent of the world's natural gas reserves and more than 90 percent of Russia's gas, Gazprom remains one of the world's largest companies. It also owns the entire pipeline infrastructure in Russia, meaning that it decides how much gas goes to domestic and export markets. In many ways Gazprom is more like an independent state than a company. It has its own bank, insurance company, and media outlets, and even owns its own soccer team in Saint Petersburg.

Factories, which under the Soviets had provided not only employment but also social services, such as child care and housing benefits, struggled to stay afloat. Yeltsin's government borrowed huge sums to keep the factories running, but this only led to more inflation. Inadequate politicians failed to set up an effective tax code, strong property rights, or coherent bankruptcy laws. Yeltsin tried to speed privatization of many industries, hoping that a thriving capitalist class would show that communism was not going to return. However, privatized businesses mostly ended up in the hands of those who had friends among Yeltsin and his government allies.

By 1999, when Yeltsin handed power to Vladimir Putin, most of Russia's economy had been privatized. The vast majority of citizens had seen their living standards fall, government services plummet, and crime and corruption explode. Budget shortfalls affected law enforcement and medical care. It was enough to make some nostalgic for the old order. "So, where are we now?" wrote the Russian journalist Anna Politkovskaya. "We who lived in the Soviet Union, where most of us had a stable job and a salary we could rely on, who had unbounded, unshakable confidence in what tomorrow would bring. . . . What kind of existence are we eking out now? What new roles have we been allocated?"[17] Widespread distrust of capitalism enabled Putin to present his government-centered program as a better alternative. The decade from 1999 to 2008 saw strong economic growth in Russia, with the gross domestic product increasing almost 7 percent annually. After the hectic years of perestroika and privatization, Russians approved of the stable economy and rise in living standards that Putin oversaw. Many seemed ready to endure authoritarian rule once more if it meant an end to uncertainty and turmoil.

> "So, where are we now? We who lived in the Soviet Union, where most of us had a stable job and a salary we could rely on, who had unbounded, unshakable confidence in what tomorrow would bring. . . . What kind of existence are we eking out now?"[17]
>
> —Anna Politkovskaya, a Russian journalist.

CHAPTER FOUR

A Society in Flux

In the decade following the collapse of the Soviet Union, the birthrate in Russia also collapsed. Low birthrates combined with an average life expectancy lower than in most European and Asian countries caused an alarming drop in population. In the 2000s the number of deaths in Russia exceeded the number of births. Experts attribute the decline to worries among young Russians about the struggling economy. (During the Great Depression of the 1930s, birthrates in the United States and Europe showed a similar decline.) Russian president Vladimir Putin has addressed the problem with pro-family policies that encourage childbearing. For example, one program pays the equivalent of $10,000 to families who have a second child. Other programs support day care centers and preschools. These policies, combined with a generally improving economy, have helped reverse the falling birthrate. Today, the birthrate in Russia is actually higher than in the United States, but the low number of births during the anxious years after the Soviet Union's fall will likely limit Russian population growth for more than a generation. Much will depend on how optimistic young Russians are about their future.

Russian Society After the October Revolution

After the Bolsheviks' October Revolution, optimism in Russia was tempered by fears about civil war, food shortages, and job security. The Bolsheviks immediately set about making changes to society based on their socialist beliefs. The most significant changes had more effect in cities, where the Bolsheviks enjoyed more support, than in the countryside, where the peasantry clung to old ways. Workers were able to vote in soviets that organized in the factories, which seemed to give them a voice regarding their working conditions. A new sense of upward mobility took hold. An individual who joined the Communist Party had new opportunities to rise in society. Many citizens felt they had a stake in society for the first time. The Bolsheviks tried to bolster these feelings by trumpeting Marxist propaganda about ending exploitation, sharing resources, and preparing for the glorious future that lay ahead.

Lenin, Trotsky, and the Bolsheviks set about transforming Russian society in the most fundamental ways. As militant atheists, the Bolsheviks promoted a hostile attitude toward religion. They strove to limit the influence of the Russian Orthodox Church, which had long played a major role in Russian society. Education focused on socialist values, such as collective purpose and productive labor. The Bolsheviks also took steps to end gender inequality. In 1918 the government passed the Code on Marriage, the Family, and Guardianship, which supporters hailed as the most progressive family legislation in the world. Marriage became strictly a civil process based on mutual consent. Divorce could be initiated by either partner. Illegitimacy was abolished, as parent-child relationships were considered separate from marriage bonds. Child-care responsibilities were transferred from the family to the state. Children of separated parents received guaranteed financial support, and women with children usually got favorable treatment in divorce proceedings. Abortion became legal at any stage in pregnancy. Gender discrimination in the workplace with regard to hiring and firing was outlawed. Household tasks, such as cooking and doing laundry, were to be performed by paid workers, enabling more women to take jobs in the public sphere.

Bolshevik philosophy sought to separate the family from its traditional social functions, causing it eventually to give way to relationships based on equality and mutual respect. In 1920 Clara Zetkin, a German revolutionary, spoke approvingly of Lenin's approach to gender equality: "Comrade Lenin repeatedly discussed with me the problem of women's rights. He obviously attached great importance to the

Bolsheviks attack a monastery and round up members of the clergy. Driven by their hostility toward religion, the Bolsheviks tried mightily to limit the influence of the Russian Orthodox Church.

women's movement, which was to him an essential component of the mass movement that in certain circumstances might become decisive. Needless to say he saw full social equality of women as a principle which no Communist could dispute."[18] Another aim was to involve more women in politics and government. The Bolsheviks tried to ensure a place for women in all organizations. While only about 10 percent of party members were female, many women made significant contributions to the revolution.

A Flowering of Avant-Garde Art

Advanced social ideas found their equivalents in the arts. In the early years of the Bolshevik takeover, revolutionary politics seemed to lead naturally to revolutionary art. While not all artists and intellectuals approved of the Bolsheviks, many found inspiration in the general fervor and optimism. Artistic movements such as futurism and constructivism included painters and sculptors who sought to express modern ideas about society in fresh ways. Novelist Maxim Gorky, whose stories set in the new regime were more traditional in style and sentiment, was probably the most widely known figure in Soviet culture. While some important Russian poets escaped to Europe after the revolution, many remained, such as Alexander Blok, Anna Akhmatova, and Marina Tsvetaeva. Blok's poem "The Twelve" expressed mixed feelings about the revolution in quasi-religious terms. Akhmatova, responding in part to new societal norms, wrote about romantic love in all its stages. Poet and playwright Vladimir Mayakovsky created futurist verse notable for its street language and wild imagery. (Lenin, whose artistic tastes were firmly traditional, thought Mayakovsky's style of writing was rubbish, and he gave orders to limit the print runs of Mayakovsky's books.)

> "Comrade Lenin repeatedly discussed with me the problem of women's rights. . . . Needless to say he saw full social equality of women as a principle which no Communist could dispute."[18]
>
> —Clara Zetkin, a German revolutionary.

Even more influential worldwide were the Russian experiments in cinema. Director Sergei Eisenstein pioneered a technique of montage—juxtaposing images in rapid succession—that is the basis for most film editing today. Eisenstein's 1925 film *Battleship Potemkin* was powerful propaganda that dramatized the sailors' mutiny in the 1905 revolution, connecting those events to the Bolsheviks' triumph. Dziga Vertov's 1929 *Man with a Movie Camera* documented urban life with imaginative images and frenetic editing that went beyond Eisenstein. The new Soviet art, with its formal experimentation and willingness to break boundaries, drew praise from intellectuals around the world. However, it had little appeal for the ordinary Russian worker.

Socialist Realism Under Stalin

When Stalin rose to power, the Communist Party moved to tighten its grip on all aspects of society, including art. The party relied heavily on mass-produced posters to reach workers in cities and towns. Art historian Victoria E. Bonnell wrote:

> As the 1930s proceeded, visual propaganda became more intensive and widespread. For the first time, in 1931, all poster production was brought under the supervision of the Art Department of the State Publishing House (Izogiz), which operated under the direct supervision of the Central Committee. Henceforth, the themes, texts, and images of posters were dictated to artists and closely regulated by official censors.[19]

"In 1931, all poster production was brought under the supervision of the Art Department of the State Publishing House. . . . Henceforth, the themes, texts, and images of posters were dictated to artists and closely regulated by official censors."[19]

—Victoria E. Bonnell, an art historian.

In 1934 the party declared socialist realism to be the required style for works of art and literature. Socialist realism sought to portray life in the Soviet Union not as it was but in its ideal form. Novelists and playwrights wrote about building steel plants or working on collective farms in a simple, sentimentalized style. Heroes tended to be patriotic, one-dimensional figures who mouthed praises for the party and its Five-Year Plans. Government censorship ensured that socialist realism was practically the only style of art that reached the public. Some novelists rewrote their books to conform to the censors. Serious writers, such as Mikhail Bulgakov and Isaac Babel, who wanted to explore life without restrictions or ideological guidelines, had difficulty publishing their work. Any experiments in style were condemned as elitist—not suitable for the enjoyment of ordinary people. The state preferred painters and illustrators who created sentimental images of

Alexandra Kollontai, Bolshevik Feminist

A major voice for socialism and feminism, Alexandra Kollontai tried to create new roles for women in the Soviet Union. Born in 1872 to a wealthy Saint Petersburg family, Kollontai showed an early gift for languages, which proved useful in her revolutionary work. As a young mother, she helped educate and organize working-class women in evening classes. In 1905 she began to organize female workers in Russia and encourage them to press for their rights in the workplace and in bourgeois society. In 1908, facing an arrest warrant for her underground activities, Kollontai fled into European exile. In 1917 she returned to Russia to lead strikes of women workers. When the Bolsheviks seized power, Kollontai was named Commissar of Social Welfare in the new government. In 1919 she became head of the newly created women's section of the Communist Party. She led efforts to educate Soviet women about new laws on labor, marriage, and education.

However, disillusionment began to set in, and she joined a workers' opposition movement that branded her as a possible troublemaker. From 1922 until her retirement in 1945, Kollontai served outside the country in various diplomatic posts. "Even while she was earning her decorations she was in fear for her life," wrote Clive James, a critic and documentarian. During the purges of the late 1930s, he continued, "she thought every trip back to Moscow might be her last." In virtual exile as a diplomat, Kollontai saw her views on women's rights lose support. Yet many modern-day feminists view Kollontai as a courageous pioneer.

Clive James, *Cultural Amnesia: Necessary Memories from History and the Arts.* New York: Norton, 2007, p. 362.

"Father Stalin" visiting factory workers or receiving a bouquet of roses from admiring children. The main challenge for Soviet writers and artists was keeping up with the current party line. One misstep could be fatal.

Some indeed paid for their art with their lives. In 1933 Osip Mandelstam, a talented poet, was arrested for writing a poem that ridiculed Stalin. The poem described the dictator's "fingers . . . fat as grubs" and "cockroach whiskers" and declared that for Stalin, "every killing is a treat."[20] After first being exiled, Mandelstam was eventually sent to the Gulag, where he died in 1938. Babel, whose book of stories titled *Red Cavalry* is a masterpiece of realistic war fiction, fell victim to Stalin's purges and was shot in January

The Russian poet Osip Mandelstam (pictured) was arrested and exiled for writing a poem that ridiculed Stalin. Mandelstam was eventually imprisoned in the Gulag, where he died in 1938.

1940. Theater director Vsevolod Meyerhold was arrested for "spying" for foreign governments. Meyerhold described his plight in a letter written just before his execution: "The investigators began to use force on me, a sick 65-year-old man. . . . I howled and wept from the pain. I incriminated myself in the hope that by telling them lies I could end the ordeal."[21]

A Regimented Society

Soviet society under Stalin featured increasing regimentation and rigid control. Children joined the *Komsomol*, or Communist Youth League, and learned in school about Stalin's glorious role in the revolution. Adults took part in the approved party organizations, read state-approved newspapers, and listened to state-approved music. Most families lived in tiny apartments with scant amenities. Few people kept diaries or journals for fear they would fall into the wrong hands. Religious practice was curtailed as churches were demolished and church leaders arrested. Health care was available for all, but while the number of qualified doctors increased, so too did state control over their practices. Workers were allowed vacations—unheard of in czarist times—and the state provided facilities for games and exercise. However, there was a general atmosphere of anxiety in the years of the purges.

Even during the partial thaw of the Khrushchev years, personal freedom was extremely limited for most citizens. Only an elite group of party functionaries was allowed to travel outside the country. Movement inside the Soviet Union was also restricted, with few rural farmworkers allowed to migrate to cities. The KGB, or secret police, maintained a widespread surveillance network to ferret out any signs of disloyalty or dissension. An army of informants reported the slightest deviation from appropriate behavior. Soviet citizens came to assume that every room was bugged, every phone line tapped, and every conversation recorded. The KGB compiled dossiers on anyone considered in the least suspicious. Once arrested, a detainee could be held without sleep, questioned for hours, and "reeducated" to support the party without hesitation. Possession of banned books was a crime against the state. Subversive material that could not be published was circulated in typewritten copies called *samizdat.* Communications with foreigners often had to be smuggled in and out of the country.

Government control extended even to science and technology. Since the regime defined itself as different from all others, its science had to be distinct as well. For example, Stalin supported a poorly educated scientist named Trofim Lysenko who claimed to have discovered an approach to genetics that was ideologically superior to that of Western scientists. The fact that Lysenko was completely deluded did not prevent his being lionized as a great genius by Soviet officials and his theories being taught in Soviet universities. From the 1950s to the 1980s, the Soviet Union produced many gifted scientists who made major breakthroughs in such fields as nuclear physics and satellite technology. Nevertheless, Soviet science often was subject to ideological demands and restrictions and thus lagged behind the West's.

Societal Changes Under Gorbachev and Yeltsin

Gorbachev's program to ease the Soviet government's grip on political and economic matters set in motion an avalanche of changes. The media, schools, religious groups, and small entrepreneurs enjoyed new freedoms. School administrators were urged to downplay Marxist ideology and focus instead on instilling good work habits. With the Russian media able to report more freely, people learned details about crime and corruption that had always been suppressed. Many older citizens blamed Gorbachev for the new glasnost, or openness, that revealed uncomfortable truths about the Soviet system. Exposés disclosed unhealthy working conditions for factory workers and unjust dismissals of women with small children. The swirl of revelations combined with the shaky economy, high inflation, and food shortages led to social unrest among workers. They worried that the job security and welfare programs the government had always provided were coming to an end. While some welcomed a shift toward capitalism, others feared the words "market reforms."

Yeltsin's attempt to install a market-based economy brought mixed results. Privatization mostly enriched a small number of tycoons who took control of factories, companies, and Russia's plentiful natural resources.

Sports in the Soviet Union

Like almost everything else in Soviet society, sports were organized to aid the Communist Party. After the Bolshevik Revolution, the Soviet government refused to send athletes to the International Olympic Games, claiming they were elitist, bourgeois activities. In the 1930s, however, Soviet officials began to see that success in international competitions could be an excellent propaganda tool to display the superiority of their political system. Posters urging young Soviets to train hard to achieve greatness appeared throughout the nation. The government spared no expense in scouting, training, and coaching the best athletes in Russia and the other republics.

In its forty years of Olympic competition, from 1952 to 1992, the Soviet Union enjoyed extraordinary success. Six times the Soviet Union ranked first in number of gold medals won, and it ranked second three other times. The Soviet Union's Olympic stars included sprinters, hurdlers, boxers, weight lifters, wrestlers, and gymnasts. In the 1972 Olympic Games, for example, Valery Borzov, dubbed by reporters the "Soviet Express," won the 100-meter and 200-meter dashes to become recognized as the world's fastest man. At the same Olympics, pigtailed gymnast Olga Korbut won three gold medals while enchanting viewers with her radiant smile and daring somersaults. Commentators joked that Korbut had done more for international relations than any diplomat. In other years Cold War tensions often ratcheted up the competitive spirit for Soviet athletes and their opponents. In 1956, the year that Soviet troops invaded Hungary, the two nations played an Olympic water polo match that became famous for the amount of blood in the water.

Nevertheless, many people, particularly young and ambitious city dwellers, embraced the changes. Large numbers of women quit their low-paying jobs as teachers or medical workers to sell Western brands of clothing or cosmetics. Business schools could barely keep up with the number of applicants. Parents even sent their children to modeling school in hopes they

Pedestrians in Moscow walk under a billboard advertising beauty products by L'Oréal Paris. By the mid-1990s western companies were finding new and enthusiastic markets among Russia's young, ambitious city dwellers.

would make it big in the fashion industry. Car dealerships sprang up, selling luxury vehicles. Billboards and neon signs pitched a bewildering variety of new goods. "As late as 1990," wrote David Remnick, a longtime Moscow correspondent, "a ballplayer in search of a decent pair of basketball shoes bought them on the black market, abroad, or not at all. By 1996

Nike and Reebok had outposts in Moscow, and for the summer Olympics, the main sponsor of the Russian Olympic team was no longer the Communist Party of the Soviet Union, but rather the executives of Reebok."[22]

To cater to this new consumerism, stodgy publications gave way to new versions with hipper formats. Restaurants of every description appeared on formerly rundown boulevards in Moscow and Saint Petersburg. Flights abroad were filled with giddy Russians able for the first time to visit relatives in New York City or tourist destinations in Paris and Rome. Professors of history and art were finally able to view in person the sites and works they had been writing about for years. The idea that foreign travel had so recently been forbidden to the average citizen seemed absurd.

At the same time, Russians encountered a darker side of freedom. Street crime increased at alarming rates, with muggings and car thefts a daily occurrence. Violence between gangs run by the newly rich profiteers spilled into the streets. A business owner might be eating caviar in his gated mansion one night and blown to bits by a remote-control car bomb the next. Some observers compared the new lawlessness to the 1920s in the United States, a period when bootlegging gangsters with submachine guns settled their vendettas in the streets.

Social Media in Putin's Russia

After Vladimir Putin assumed the presidency in 2000, gang-related violence was curbed, but so too were many civil rights, such as freedom of the press and the right of assembly. Yet Russians, particularly the young, increasingly are turning to the Internet and social media to trade information and express themselves. This has been a remarkable development in a nation where people traditionally are distrustful and wary of government surveillance. Only 10 percent of business transactions in Russia are conducted online, as customers fear that personal information may not be secure. Web-based businesses have to be innovative and trustworthy to succeed. Oktogo, the leading Russian site for booking travel, allows users to complete most reservations in person. The online dating service Topface has become one of the top ten Russian Internet companies by attracting more than half its users from outside Russia.

The nation's best-known online business is probably VKontakte (VK), the Russian version of Facebook, which has more than 240 million users. Its founder, Pavel Durov, became notorious for once sailing paper airplanes made from ruble banknotes out of his office window. Most controversial has been the role played by VK users in organizing protests against Putin's reelection and policies. In January 2014 Durov sold his stake in VK to a business partner of Putin's richest associate. "Of course the Kremlin wants loyal owners at VK," said Yevgeny Minchenko, a Moscow political analyst. "Putin's entourage knows the opposition could use VK's . . . users to ignite political strife."[23]

Today Russian society continues to chafe under a leadership that professes democratic values but uses any means to maintain power and control. It remains to be seen whether innovations like computer technology and social media can help the Russian people unite to bring change to their country.

> "Of course the Kremlin wants loyal owners at VK [Russia's social network site]. Putin's entourage knows the opposition could use VK's . . . users to ignite political strife."[23]
>
> —Yevgeny Minchenko, a Moscow political analyst.

CHAPTER FIVE

Russia's Future: Pitfalls and Possibilities

The former republics of the Soviet Union have been independent since 1991, yet Russian president Vladimir Putin still seeks to prevent their developing closer ties with Europe. In November 2013 Dmitry Rogozin, Putin's deputy prime minister, warned the nation of Moldova about its continued negotiations with the European Union. He hinted that Russia could cut off the supply of cheap natural gas on which Moldova depends. "Energy supplies are important in the run-up to winter," Rogozin said. "I hope you won't freeze."[24] Russia also banned imports of Moldovan wines. Putin employed similar bullying tactics with Ukraine, Georgia, Belarus, and other former Soviet republics.

Just a few months later, Putin demonstrated his concern about improving Russia's image on the eve of the 2014 Winter Olympics in Sochi. Putin released several high-profile political prisoners, including former oil executive Mikhail Khodorkovsky. Putin and his associates viewed the Sochi Olympics, for which lavish preparations had been made, as a showcase for the Russian Federation's achievements and wealth. Critics saw the moves as an attempt to obscure the true character of Putin's authoritarian regime. Most observers agree that the future of the Russian Federation is inextricably linked to Putin and his iron-fisted program of control and intimidation.

A four-man bobsled team takes a run down the track at the 2014 Winter Olympics in Sochi, Russia. Russian president Vladimir Putin viewed the Olympics as an opportunity to showcase his country's achievements and wealth.

The Rise of Putin

Putin's desire for control goes back to his years as a lieutenant colonel in the KGB. As a child living in a tiny apartment in Leningrad, Putin saw the rubble from the terrible Nazi siege of the early 1940s and heard stories about the Russian people's courage and endurance. He loved to read about Soviet agents and idolized those who worked as spies in foreign countries. Putin's classmates remember him as short in stature but prone to fistfights when crossed. He learned discipline in a judo club and improved his academics, earning a degree at a prestigious university. At age 23, he was accepted into the KGB and eventually was sent to Dresden, East Germany, where he watched with disgust as Gorbachev's reforms led to open protests, mass exodus to the West, and the end of the Soviet bloc. With his dream of being a successful spy overtaken by historical events, he returned to Leningrad with his wife and children. Like many former KGB agents, Putin felt betrayed and abandoned by his country.

During the Yeltsin period in the 1990s, Putin became assistant to Saint Petersburg's mayor, Anatoly Sobchak. Putin shared Sobchak's distaste for Western-style democracy and for many of the societal changes taking place all around. In 1998 Putin became head of the FSB, the secret police organization that replaced the Soviet KGB. By decade's end, with Yeltsin approaching his final weeks as president, the optimism that had greeted his push for political and economic freedom had turned to widespread disillusionment. Yeltsin had lost the public's trust, and he and his besieged inner circle were searching for a successor. They hoped to stave off the rising tide of reactionaries and former Communists who were bent on returning Russia to socialist-based authoritarian rule.

One of Yeltsin's advisers, a fabulously rich entrepreneur and media mogul named Boris Berezovsky, had a suggestion for his replacement. Berezovsky recalled an official in Saint Petersburg named Putin who had refused to accept the usual bribe during a business transaction. Yeltsin and his people knew little about Putin, only that he had been in the KGB, had remained loyal to Yeltsin throughout the recent turmoil, and was supposedly Berezovsky's protégé. They assumed Putin was a lightweight politician who would be easy to guide in the right direction. Besides, Putin looked dapper in his European-made suits, the very image of the new Russia that Yeltsin wanted to promote. It was on this basis that Putin was handed leadership of the world's largest country in land area and the producer of vast amounts of the world's oil and natural gas.

However, Putin promptly demonstrated that he was no figurehead leader. Responding to a series of apartment house bombings in Moscow and other Russian cities in the summer of 1999, Putin appeared on Russian TV. He blamed the violence on rebels from the Muslim-dominated Chechnya region and vowed to use military force to crush them. The Russian public approved of this confident, tough-talking politician who refused to mince words. "Putin was using rhetoric markedly different from Yeltsin's," according to Masha Gessen, a Russian journalist and editor. "He was not promising to bring the terrorists to justice. Nor was he expressing compassion for the hundreds of victims of the explosions. This was the language of a leader who was planning to rule with his fist."[25]

Putin authorized immediate bombing raids on Grozny, the main Chechen city, and also sent troops to the area despite laws against using them inside Russia's borders. Subsequent reports suggested that the apartment bombings had actually been carried out by the FSB, Putin's old agency, but it seemed to make little difference to the electorate. A few months after the bombings, Putin easily won election as president of the Russian Federation. He has continued in power ever since. Some Russians still see him as a romantic adventurer, throwing a judo master over his shoulder or riding a horse shirtless through the steppe. Others see him as a reactionary bully, intent only on bending adversaries to his will. Regardless, the future of Russia for years to come—politically, economically, socially—will doubtless be stamped by his authoritarian rule.

> "Putin was using rhetoric markedly different from Yeltsin's. . . . This was the language of a leader who was planning to rule with his fist."[25]
>
> —Masha Gessen, a Russian journalist and editor.

Russia's Political Future

There is no prospect for Western-style democracy in Russia as long as Putin remains in power. From the start, he has made sure to eliminate anyone who might become a potent political rival or troublesome critic. In 2003 he authorized the arrest of oil billionaire Mikhail Khodorkovsky on charges of tax evasion and embezzlement. Observers at the time suspected that Khodorkovsky's real crime was arguing for social justice in Russia and blaming Putin for a stagnant economy. Another thwarted opposition leader was Alexei Navalny, a lawyer and charismatic politician arrested in 2009, also for embezzlement. Alexander Litvinenko, an FSB agent who accused Putin of staging the notorious Moscow apartment bombings that led to the Second Chechen War, was dealt with even more harshly. Litvinenko died in a London hospital bed, poisoned by a radioactive substance called polonium.

Foreign politicians could also be targets. In 2004 the reform candidate for the Ukrainian presidency, Viktor Yushchenko, suffered a poisonous attack

Putin on the Role of Government in the Economy

The 2008 credit crisis in the United States affected all nations. The Russian Federation, with its economy based on energy exports, was hit particularly hard. In a speech in Davos, Switzerland, on January 27, 2009, Vladimir Putin addressed the financial crisis and the role of government in dealing with it.

> Excessive intervention in economic activity and blind faith in the state's omnipotence is another possible mistake. True, the state's increased role in times of crisis is a natural reaction to market setbacks. Instead of streamlining market mechanisms, some are tempted to expand state economic intervention to the greatest possible extent. . . . In the 20th century, the Soviet Union made the state's role absolute. In the long run, this made the Soviet economy totally uncompetitive. This lesson cost us dearly. I am sure nobody wants to see it repeated. Nor should we turn a blind eye to the fact that the spirit of free enterprise, including the principle of personal responsibility of businesspeople, investors and shareholders for their decisions, is being eroded in the last few months. There is no reason to believe that we can achieve better results by shifting responsibility onto the state.

Although Putin's remarks suggest the need for governments to show restraint, his government has often intervened in the Russian economy.

Quoted in *Wall Street Journal*, "Putin Speaks at Davos," January 28, 2009. http://online.wsj.com.

that caused his face to break out in disfiguring cysts and pustules. Yushchenko survived to finally win the election. Still, many suspected that Putin—who had staunchly supported Yushchenko's opponent in the race—was behind the poisoning. Putin certainly opposed Yushchenko's plans to develop closer ties between Ukraine and the West. Such concerns were the main reason Putin invaded the former Soviet republic of Georgia in 2008 and also lay behind his seizure of Crimea and the veiled threats to Ukraine in 2014. Journalists who speak out against Putin's aggression risk being silenced. The writer and human rights activist Anna Politkovskaya received numerous death threats for her books and articles about Putin's brutal policies in the Chechen conflict. On October 7, 2006, she was found murdered in her Moscow apartment building.

Such incidents show the price of crossing Putin. Like their president, most Russians treat American ideas about democracy with skepticism. This attitude allows Putin and his circle to focus on centralized control and downplay any need for democratic reforms. Some analysts, looking for reasons to be optimistic, point to an increase in political competition, but this is mainly within Putin's ruling party. Others fear that the ease with which Putin has maintained power is evidence that things are getting worse politically. For example, Putin recently has shown signs of cracking down even further on free expression. In January 2014 David Satter, an adviser to the US-backed radio service Radio Liberty, was expelled from Russia. "The Russian decision to declare me persona non grata," Satter wrote, "is more than an action against a single journalist. It is an admission that the system under President Vladimir Putin cannot tolerate free speech, even in the case of foreign correspondents."[26]

> "The Russian decision to declare me persona non grata . . . is an admission that the system under President Vladimir Putin cannot tolerate free speech, even in the case of foreign correspondents."[26]
>
> —David Satter, an adviser to the radio service Radio Liberty, who was expelled from Russia.

Prospects for Russia's Economy

Putin's government has had a mixed record regarding economic freedom. Soon after taking office, Putin made a deal with the corporate leaders who had benefited from Yeltsin's privatization policies: He would not interfere with their businesses as long as they agreed to stay out of politics. At the

Russian soldiers unload tanks at a Crimean railway station in March 2014. Russia defied Ukrainian government opposition when it annexed Crimea, a region of southeastern Ukraine, after residents of Crimea voted for annexation.

same time he seized control of the broadcast media. As Russia's economy boomed due to rising oil prices, the oligarchs (wealthy owners of corporations) became even richer and more beholden to the state. Regardless of his promises, Putin did not hesitate to step in when he saw the need. One example occurred in 2004 when Russia's largest oil company, Yukos, was offered for sale to a Western buyer. Putin arrested its executives, including Khodorkovsky, forced the firm into bankruptcy, and sold off the company's assets to political allies. Putin has kept oversight of other large companies either by buying majority ownership, as with Gazprom, or by placing friends on corporate boards, often as the chair. Under Putin, the government has amassed a shareholding portfolio equal to 40 percent of the Russian stock market. According to the World Bank, the country's twenty-three largest companies account for 30 percent of Russia's annual economic output, and these companies are controlled by only thirty-seven individuals.

Lenin's Mausoleum

A symbol of the difficulty Russia has in escaping its past is Lenin's Mausoleum in Red Square. Inside lies Lenin's corpse, meticulously mummified by a team of scientists ninety years ago. The body has been on continuous display since shortly after the dictator's death in 1924, except for a four-year period during World War II when it was evacuated to Siberia. The idea of embalming Lenin originated with Stalin. Reportedly, Lenin's widow, Nadezhda Krupskaya, bitterly opposed the notion, preferring her husband to be honored by the building of schools and hospitals. Nevertheless, Stalin and other party leaders decided to create a "cult of Lenin." They held a grandiose national funeral and changed the name of Petrograd to Leningrad.

In 2013 the mausoleum site was closed several months for renovations, but once again it is open to the public. A survey in December 2012 found that three-fourths of Russians thought Lenin's corpse should be removed from display and buried in the Kremlin or in Saint Petersburg. "I don't think Lenin should still be here, on display though, to be honest," said Natalia, a twenty-four-year-old visitor to the site. "He's part of our history, but a bad part. There is so much negative energy radiating from that coffin."

Quoted in Shaun Walker, "Vladimir Lenin Is Once Again on Display to Visitors in Moscow's Red Square as Mausoleum Reopens," *Independent* (London), May 15, 2013. www.independent .co.uk.

Despite this concentration, the Russian economy under Putin has thrived in many ways. In 2001 Putin reformed the tax system, replacing the old higher rates with a flat tax of 13 percent. Payroll taxes also were cut. Under Putin, average income has nearly doubled, and a new stability has resulted in a growing middle class. He has increased pensions and the salaries of police and civil servants. The unemployment rate has remained low, with more than one-quarter of all workers employed by the state. Putin's environmental record, however, has been mostly a disappointment. Despite publicity stunts, such as tagging endangered gray whales using a crossbow, Putin has been slow to address problems in managing waterways, forests, and air quality. He has also harassed environmental organizations that have been critical of his policies, requiring them to register as foreign agents and looking into their operations.

The Future of Russian Society

Through the years Putin has grown increasingly conservative in his social outlook, which is reflected in the nation's laws and how they are enforced. Putin and his allies, along with officials of the Orthodox Church, promote what to them are traditional Russian family values. Often this results in protests from feminists or supporters of civil rights. For example, under the Russian criminal code, domestic violence is rarely punished and women have few legal safeguards. Government statistics indicate that one-fourth of Russian women report sexual or physical abuse in the home. Nevertheless, traditionalists insist that the state should not meddle in marital quarrels. "Russia is behind when it comes to legal protection for women—it doesn't have the basic parameters that women need to be protected from domestic abuse," said Gauri van Gulik, a Berlin-based representative for Human Rights Watch. "The economic costs of domestic violence are incredibly high, so it's not just important for women, it's important for the development of the country itself."[27] A new domestic violence bill has been proposed, but the Putin government has been noncommittal, and Orthodox Church leaders have called the bill antifamily. In an attempt to strengthen what Putin calls the Russian identity, his supporters have proposed raising a tax on divorce to more than $900 and offering cash incentives for couples to have at least three children. Putin's government has also imposed antigay laws that have drawn protests from gay activists around

> "Russia is behind when it comes to legal protection for women—it doesn't have the basic parameters that women need to be protected from domestic abuse."[27]
>
> —Gauri van Gulik, a Berlin-based representative for Human Rights Watch.

Masked members of the Russian punk rock band Pussy Riot leave a Sochi police station in February 2014. Police said the women were arrested in connection with a theft, but band members believe they are being harassed because of their public opposition to Vladimir Putin's policies.

the world. An all-female punk rock band, Pussy Riot, arose in opposition to what they saw as an alliance between Putin and the Orthodox Church. In March 2012 the band was arrested and two of its members sent to jail for what the court called hooliganism motivated by religious hatred. Putin had the women released in December 2013.

Government harassment aside, Russian society offers more opportunities for women than ever before. Women are starting their own businesses in record numbers, and they own a majority of small businesses, many of them Internet-based. Yet Russian females still face major hurdles to success in the corporate world. While women hold more than 13 percent of senior managerial posts in Europe's large companies, the corresponding number in Russia is only 7 percent. Women's organizations hope that more Russian women will run for political office and promote legislation to improve the lot of females in society. The Russian Federation ranks ninety-sixth in the world in percentage of parliamentary seats occupied by women, with only 13.3 percent.

Like women in Russia, ethnic and religious minorities face new opportunities and challenges. Growth in the number of Muslims promises unforeseen changes to Russian society. Today's 23 million Muslims make up about 15 percent of Russia's total population, but that proportion is growing rapidly. Birthrates for Muslim women are more than twice that of ethnic Russians. Analysts expect Muslims to make up almost half the Russian army within a few years. This could present challenges in military operations against Muslims in Russia, like the war in Chechnya. Religious-based tensions have broken out as recently as October 2013, when the stabbing murder of an ethnic Russian by a Muslim native of the Caucasus resulted in vandalism and rioting in Moscow. Putin has often emphasized that the Russian Federation is a secular state and has, for example, opposed the wearing of Islamic head scarves in Russian schools.

A Nation of Contradictions

For all their diversity in customs and beliefs, the Russian people share a passion for life that is unmistakable. But they are also a people filled with contradictions. Many travelers have remarked on the cold demeanor of Russian officials and the surliness of waiters, while others see a warm and generous side to the Russian character that is reflected in a love of celebration and gift giving. The cliché of the dark Russian soul prone to brooding over poetry and the meaning of life also has an element of truth. Some have said that only a strong ruler—the *silnaya ruka*—can overcome the people's contradictory nature and lack of discipline and bring order to Russia's inherent chaos. Under czars, fanatical revolutionaries, and modern authoritarians, the Russian people have suffered and endured. Like the czarist symbol of the two-headed eagle, the Russian Federation today looks partially toward the autocratic traditions of the East and partially toward the democratic ideals of the West. For now, the Russian people seem content to navigate their own unique path between these two sets of ideas.

SOURCE NOTES

Introduction: The Russian Federation

1. Quoted in CBS News, "Putin: Snowden Must Stop 'Damaging Our American Partners,'" July 1, 2013. www.cbsnews.com.
2. Robert M. Gates, "Putin's Challenge to the West," *Wall Street Journal*, March 25, 2014. http://online.wsj.com.
3. Mark Adomanis, "Five Myths About Russia," *Forbes*, February 4, 2013. www.forbes.com.

Chapter One: The October Revolution

4. Quoted in History in an Hour, "The October Revolution—a Summary,'" November 7, 2012. www.historyinanhour.com.
5. Quoted in Bertram D. Wolfe, *Three Who Made a Revolution*. New York: Dell, 1964, p. 31.
6. Richard Pipes, *Communism: A History*. New York: Modern Library, 2001, p. 39.
7. Quoted in Robert C. Tucker, ed., *The Lenin Anthology*. New York: Norton, 1975, p. 727.

Chapter Two: A Tradition of Tyranny

8. Robert Conquest, *Stalin: Breaker of Nations*. New York: Viking Penguin, 1991, p. 180.
9. Conquest, *Stalin,* p. 236.
10. Samuel Rachlin, "Stalin's Long Shadow," *New York Times*, March 4, 2013. www.nytimes.com.
11. Martin Sixsmith, *Russia: A 1,000-Year Chronicle of the Wild East*. New York: Overlook, 2011, pp. 452–53.
12. David Remnick, *Lenin's Tomb: The Last Days of the Soviet Empire*. New York: Random House, 1993, p. 490.
13. Quoted in Stephen K. Wegren, ed., *Return to Putin's Russia: Past Imperfect, Future Uncertain,* 5th ed. Lanham, MD: Rowman & Littlefield, 2013, p. 11.

Chapter Three: From Communism to Free Markets

14. John McCain, "Russians Deserve Better than Putin," *Pravda*, September 19, 2013. http://english.pravda.ru.
15. Quoted in Douglas Smith, *Former People: The Final Days of the Russian Aristocracy.* New York: Farrar, Straus & Giroux, 2012. p. 5.
16. Quoted in Mount Holyoke College, "Soviet Russia: Class Extermination Under Stalin." www.mholyoke.edu.
17. Anna Politkovskaya, *Putin's Russia: Life in a Failing Democracy.* New York: Holt, 2004, p. 81.

Chapter Four: A Society in Flux

18. Quoted in Tucker, *The Lenin Anthology,* p. 685.
19. Victoria E. Bonnell, *Iconography of Power: Soviet Political Posters Under Lenin and Stalin.* Berkeley and Los Angeles: University of California Press, 1997, p. 6.
20. Quoted in Nadezhda Mandelstam, *Hope Against Hope: A Memoir.* New York: Modern Library, 1999, p. 13.
21. Quoted in Pipes, *Communism,* p. 63.
22. David Remnick, *Resurrection: The Struggle for a New Russia.* New York: Random House, 1997, p. 161.
23. Quoted in Irina Reznik, "Fish Tie Kremlin to New Owner of Facebook's Russian Rival," *Global Tech* (blog), Bloomberg News, June 26, 2013. www.bloomberg.com.

Chapter Five: Russia's Future: Pitfalls and Possibilities

24. Quoted in *Chicago Tribune*, "Russia Warns Moldova over Its Pro-Europe Push," September 3, 2013. http://articles.chicagotribune.com.
25. Masha Gessen, *The Man Without a Face: The Unlikely Rise of Vladimir Putin.* New York: Riverhead, 2012, pp. 26–27.
26. David Satter, "Why Journalists Frighten Putin," *Wall Street Journal*, January 15, 2014. http://online.wsj.com.
27. Quoted in Henry Meyer and Ksenia Galouchko, "Putin Allies Let Abuse Law Linger Despite Killings," Bloomberg News, October 28, 2013. www.bloomberg.com.

FACTS ABOUT THE RUSSIAN FEDERATION

Geography

- The Russian Federation is located in North Asia, bordering the Arctic Ocean and extending from Europe west of the Urals to the North Pacific Ocean.
- It has the largest total land area in the world, more than 6.5 million square miles (17 million sq. km).
- Its land area is approximately 1.8 times that of the United States.
- Summers vary from warm in the steppes to cool on the Arctic coast; winters vary from cool on the Black Sea to frigid in Siberia.
- Lake Baikal, the world's deepest lake, holds an estimated one-fifth of the world's freshwater.

People and Society

- The official language is Russian, with many minor languages.
- The population is estimated at more than 142.5 million, the tenth highest in the world.
- 72.5 percent of the population is age 25 or older, with a median age of 38.8 years.
- The birthrate of 12.1 births per 1,000 ranks 165th in the world.
- The life expectancy at birth of 69.85 years ranks 152nd in the world.
- Males have an average life expectancy of 64.04 years and females of 76.02 years.

Government

- The Russian capital is Moscow.
- The national symbols are the bear and the double-headed eagle.
- The name of the country in the native language is Rossiyskaya Federatsiya.
- The country achieved independence from the Soviet Union on August 24, 1991.
- The right to vote is universal beginning at age eighteen.

Economy

- The 2012 estimated gross domestic product (GDP) was $2.486 trillion (in US dollars); ranked seventh in the world.
- The 2012 estimated GDP growth rate was 3.4 percent; ranked one hundredth in the world.
- The 2012 estimated GDP per capita was $17,500; ranked seventy-eighth in the world.
- The 2012 estimated unemployment rate was 5.5 percent; ranked fifty-third in the world.
- The labor force by occupation consists of

  agriculture: 7.9 percent

  industry: 27.4 percent

  services: 64.7 percent

Energy

- The 2012 estimated crude oil production was 10.4 million barrels per day; ranked third in the world.
- The 2012 estimated crude oil exports were 4.69 million barrels per day; ranked second in the world.
- The 2013 estimated crude oil proven reserves were 80 billion barrels; ranked eighth in the world.
- The 2012 estimated natural gas production was 23.8 trillion cubic feet (673.2 billion cu. m); ranked second in the world.
- The 2012 estimated natural gas exports were 7 trillion cubic feet (198.2 billion cu. m); ranked first in the world.

Communications

- In 2012 there were 42.9 million main-line telephones in use; ranked sixth in the world.
- In 2012 there were 261.9 million mobile cellular telephones in use; ranked fifth in the world.
- In 2012 there were 14.9 million Internet hosts; ranked tenth in the world.

- In 2009 there were 40.9 million Internet users; ranked tenth in the world.
- There are an estimated thirty-three hundred national, regional, and local TV stations, more than two-thirds of which are completely or partially controlled by federal or local government.

Transportation

- The number of airports in 2013 was 1,218; ranked fifth in the world.
- The number of heliports in 2013 was forty-nine; ranked fifth in the world.
- There is a total of 54,157 miles (87,157 km) of railways; ranked second in the world.
- There is a total of 797,460 miles (1.3 million km) of roadways; ranked fifth in the world.
- There is a total of 63,380 miles (102,000 km) of navigable waterways; ranked second in the world.

Military

- Military expenditures in 2012 amounted to 4.47 percent of the GDP; ranked twenty-fourth in the world.
- In 2013 the total manpower available for military service included 34.1 million males aged sixteen to forty-nine and 35 million females aged sixteen to forty-nine.
- In 2013 the total manpower fit for military service included 20.4 million males aged sixteen to forty-nine and 26.4 million females aged sixteen to forty-nine.
- Males register for the draft at age seventeen; they must be eighteen to twenty-seven to volunteer, and their service obligation is one year with six months' training required for assignment to combat zones.

FOR FURTHER RESEARCH

Books

Simon Sebag Montefiore, *Stalin: The Court of the Red Tsar*. New York: Vintage, 2005.

Richard Pipes, *A Concise History of the Russian Revolution*. New York: Vintage, 1996.

Anna Politkovskaya, *Putin's Russia*. New York: Holt, 2004.

David Satter, *It Was a Long Time Ago, and It Never Happened Anyway: Russia and the Communist Past*. New Haven, CT: Yale University Press, 2013.

Daniel Treisman, *The Return: Russia's Journey from Gorbachev to Medvedev*. New York: Free Press, 2011.

Websites

Glasnost and Perestroika, Alpha History (http://alphahistory.com/cold war/glasnost-and-perestroika). This site explores Gorbachev's major reforms and why they led to the collapse of the Soviet Union.

Gulag, Museum on Communism (www.thegulag.org). This site includes a variety of features about the Soviet prison camp system, including maps, a time line, essays, and videos.

Joseph Stalin, Spartacus Educational (www.spartacus.schoolnet.co.uk /RUSstalin.htm). This site presents a biography of Stalin, with links to related topics about the Soviet dictator.

Profile: Vladimir Putin, BBC (www.bbc.co.uk/news/world-europe -15047823). This site looks at the life and career of the Russian Federation's president.

Russian Intelligentsia and the Bolshevik Revolution, *History Today* (www.historytoday.com/christopher-read/russian-intelligentsia-and -bolshevik-revolution). This site features a detailed look at the aftermath of the Russian Revolution and the struggle for the mind of the new Soviet citizen.

Russian Revolution in Color (www.smithsonianchannel.com/sc/web /series/1000215/russian-revolution-in-color). This two-part video documentary about the Russian Revolution depicts how workers' protests turned into full-blown social upheaval.

The Unknown Russia: Dissolving the Myths, Russiapedia (http://rus siapedia.rt.com). This site includes facts about Russian geography, history, culture, and famous people.

Vladimir Lenin, Bio.com (www.biography.com/people/vladimir-lenin -9379007). This site features a detailed biography of Lenin and a brief video of the key events in his career as a revolutionary.